Muhammed Fadhel Al-Azzawy

Translating Arabic Zoomorphic Expressions into English

Muhammed Fadhel Al-Azzawy

Translating Arabic Zoomorphic Expressions into English

A Socio-Cultural Study

Noor Publishing

Imprint

Any brand names and product names mentioned in this book are subject to trademark, brand or patent protection and are trademarks or registered trademarks of their respective holders. The use of brand names, product names, common names, trade names, product descriptions etc. even without a particular marking in this work is in no way to be construed to mean that such names may be regarded as unrestricted in respect of trademark and brand protection legislation and could thus be used by anyone.

Cover image: www.ingimage.com

Publisher:
Noor Publishing
is a trademark of
Dodo Books Indian Ocean Ltd., member of the OmniScriptum S.R.L Publishing group
str. A.Russo 15, of. 61, Chisinau-2068, Republic of Moldova Europe
Printed at: see last page
ISBN: 978-620-3-85803-7

Translating Arabic Zoomorphic Expressions into English:
A Socio-Cultural Study

by

Muhammed Fadhil Mahmood

بسم الله الرحمن الرحيم

(وَتَفَقَّدَ الطَّيْرَ فَقَالَ مَا لِيَ لا أَرَى الْهُدْهُدَ أَمْ كَانَ مِنَ الْغَائِبِينَ)

(سورة النمل ، الجزء 27, الاية : 20)

(AND HE TOOK A MUSTER OF THE BIRDS; AND HE SAID: "WHY IS IT I SEE NOT THE HOOPOE? OR IS HE AMONG THE ABSENTEES?")

(Surah Al-Naml, Chapter 27, Aya 20)

Dedication

To the soul of my late father and brother
To all my family
And friends

To the soul of my late father and brother

ACKNOWLEDGEMENTS

First of all, thanks for Allah for allowing me to start, develop and conclude this thesis. Also I would like to thank Asst. Prof. Osama H. Ibraheem ,who has successfully guided me in the development of this work, and who gave me key feedback which led me to the happy conclusion of this work. Also, I thank Asst. Prof. Essam T. Muhammed for the invaluable remarks and consistent encouragement.

I would like to extend my thanks to all the teaching staff of the Translation Department at Mosul University for collaborating with the information and patience so that I could develop this work and collect the necessary information. Many thanks to everyone who helped me in acquiring translation knowledge and the vision necessary to develop this work.

PRELUDE

Dealing with zoomorphic expressions (animal connotations) is one of the most difficult areas in the field of translation. No doubt, the way that each culture uses its language depends upon a variety of factors such as traditions, philosophical thoughts, daily activities, social systems... etc. Using language for shaping the world varies from one language to another, particularly in the use of animal connotations. Hence, the problem arises since each expression is loaded with more than one culturally variant meaning. Translators might not know whether to directly transfer what is said or written to TL or to probe into TL culture to find discrepancy between the two cultures in order to provide a suitable counterpart image. This study is an attempt to bridge this gap.

The present study mainly aims at: (1) giving a comprehensive study of zoomorphic expressions in English and Arabic, (2) testing the translatability of the zoomorphic expressions in question which are culturally and genetically different, (3) showing how the connotation of these expressions in the SL (Arabic) are different from those in the TL (English) in the light of translation, (4) detecting the causes of differences between the connotations of zoomorphic expressions in Arabic and English, and (5) specifying the method of translation that has been used by the subjects and the difficulties that they have faced.

In order to achieve these aims, the study hypothesizes that (1) zoomorphic expressions in Arabic cannot be successfully translated into English without grasping cultural values, variations and genetic associations of each culture, (2) overlooking the cultural difference between the two languages results in different renderings, (3) good decision making on the part of the translators help to arrive at what the culture-bound zoomorphic expressions under investigation implicate.

To test the validity of these hypotheses, the following procedures have been adopted: (1) a corpus of 15 Arabic examples involving zoomorphic expressions are derived from various Arabic authentic books of rhetoric, (2) these examples are translated by 8 subjects (MA students in the Department of Translation / College of Arts / University of Mosul), and (3) these zoomorphic expressions are analyzed in terms of type of figurative form (i.e. simile, proverbs, metonymy and metaphor). The main conclusions the study has arrived at: (1) lack of cultural background on the part of the subjects results in misinterpretation of the zoomorphic expressions in question and thus mistranslating the connotative meaning, (2) transferring the SL image into TL without any consideration to the lack of cultural overlap between SL and TL leads to faulty resultant translation (3) the high percentage of using foreignization (25) cases (20%) vs. Domestication (95) instances (80 %) reveals that the majority of the subjects are unaware of the cultural values that play a very important role in the process of translation.

The study ends with some recommendations for pedagogical purposes and some suggestions for further studies.

LIST OF ABBREVIATIONS

No.	Abbreviated forms	Full forms
1.	APT	Appropriate
2.	Ar.	Arabic
3.	Cor.	Correct
4.	Fig. L	Figurative Language
5.	Fig.	Figure
6.	Inc.	Incorrect
7.	Sub.	Subject
8.	SC	Source Culture
9.	SL	Source Language
10.	Sub. R	Subject Rendition
11.	ST	Source Text
12.	T.C.	Target Culture.
13.	T.L.	Target Language
14.	T.T.	Target Text
15.	ZE.	Zoomorphic Expression

LIST OF TABLES

No.	Title	page
1.	*(2-1): The Difference Between En. and Ar. Connotative Expressions*	
2.	*(3-1): Comprehensive Analytical Table of Subjects' Translations of Text One*	
3.	*(3-2): Comprehensive Analytical Table of Subjects' Translations of Text Two*	
4.	*(3-3): Comprehensive Analytical Table of Subjects' Translations of Text Three*	
5.	*(3-4): Comprehensive Analytical Table of Subjects' Translations of Text Three*	
6.	*(3-5): Comprehensive Analytical Table of Subjects' Translations of Text Four*	
7.	*(3-6): Comprehensive Analytical Table of Subjects' Translations of Text Five*	
8.	*(3-7): Comprehensive Analytical Table of Subjects' Translations of Text Six*	
9.	*(3-8): Comprehensive Analytical Table of Subjects' Translations of Text Seven*	
10.	*(3-9): Comprehensive analytical table of subjects' translations of Text Eight*	
11.	*(3-10): Comprehensive Analytical Table of Subjects' Translations of Text Nine*	
12.	*(3-11): Comprehensive Analytical Table of Subjects' Translations of Text Ten*	
13.	*(3-12): Comprehensive Analytical Table of Subjects' Translations of Text Eleven*	
14.	*(3-13): Comprehensive Analytical Table of Subjects' Translations of Text Twelve*	
15.	*(3-14): Comprehensive Analytical Table of Subjects' Translations of Text Thirteen*	
16.	*(3-15): Comprehensive Analytical Table of Subjects' Translations of Text Fourteen*	
17.	*(3-16): Total Description of Data under Study*	

LIST OF FIGURES

LIST OF CHARTS

TABLE OF CONTENTS

CHAPTER ONE

INTRODUCTION

1.1 Statement of the Problem:

This study tries to answer the following questions, which constitute the problem of the current study:

1. Does the context have any role in determining the exact connotative meaning of each word or not?

2. Do animals in English have the same connotation or symbolism as in Arabic or do they have different connotations and why?

3. What are the strategies and procedures that would be followed by the respondent translators to translate the Arabic zoomorphic expressions into English and will they all follow the same strategies and procedures or will everyone have their own?

1.2 Aims of the Study:

The current study introduces a general framework about the concept of zoomorphism both in Arabic and English cultures explaining various aspects related to this linguistic phenomenon. Similarly, an attempt is made to shed light on the problems of translating Arabic zoomorphic expressions connotative meaning into English. Since the two languages are very different from each other, the respondent translators are expected to face many problems in their attempt to translate such expressions. Since connotation is a culture- specific meaning and each culture has its connotations, one-to-one correspondence will make the translators delve into some pitfall and drawbacks here and there. Finally, the study also aims at providing the best translational strategies suitable for such culturally laden expressions.

1.3 Hypotheses:

The current study puts forward the following hypotheses:

1. It is hypothesized that the translator has to make a recognizable shift in connotation when s/he translates from Arabic in to English. This shift is because what has a negative or positive connotation in English culture does not necessarily have the same connotation in Arabic and vice versa.
2. In many cases, SL. connotation does not fit the TL context and consequently, the output translation seems awkward and ambiguous.
3. Neglecting Ar-En connotation consideration has a vital impact on the quality of translation, i.e. the produced rendering can be unclear and ambiguous for TL readers.

1.4 The Model:

Usually the model of the study is not selected haphazardly, but rather the model poses itself relying on certain parameters that will be explained further in its due section in chapter two (see the section on the adopted model of the study 2.13.1). The study supports adopting Venuti's domestication and foreignization translational method for translation such culturally laden expressions and phrases.

1.5 Data Collection and Procedures:

To achieve the goals of the study, (15) sentences have been selected with Arabic animal connotations to be distributed to MA candidates at the Department of Translation / College of Arts - Mosul University / academic year 2018-2019. the students were asked to translate the whole sentences that include zoomorphic expressions into English. After that; the renderings produced by these students will be the data of the study. The renderings then will be analyzed thoroughly according to Venuti's foreignization and domestication model of translation to find the main difficulties and problems faced by these translators in their attempt to find the appropriate equivalents of such zoomorphic expressions in English. The procedures and the strategies followed by the respondents will be discussed in detail to figure out which one is the best according to the strategies followed by these translators, then a proposed rendering is given by the researcher in case of total failure on the part of the respondent translators.

1.6 Scope of the Study:

This study is concerned with the notion of giving the attributes of animals to human beings depending on the notion of connotation and the implied meaning each animal holds. This meaning in many cases is not universal instead it is specific to a certain culture or society. This study does not depend on direct physical similarities between two objects in shape as simile does in many cases. The study also focuses on those connotations, i.e., (negative or positive) that require from the translator more efforts to find what suits ST zoomorphic expressions. The study does not limit itself to simile but also views many examples of metaphor, proverbs and metonymy in which zoomorphic connotations are used. These figurative classes will form the data.

1.7 Value of the Study:

The present study, to the best of my knowledge, is the first attempt to study the translation of English zoomorphic expressions. Hence, it will be of great benefit to the translators, especially in literary genre. It is also expected to be useful for the translation instructors and researchers in terms of investigating the field of zoomorphic expressions.

This study provides the students and teachers of translation with a critical view of the traditional theories of *metaphor, simile, metonymy* on the one hand, and a descriptive analysis of the cognitive theory of metaphor on the other hand. Similarly, it is expected for this study to be of considerable significance to those who are interested in comparative and cultural studies, since it provides a solid background knowledge about the cultural-linguistic aspects of language.

CHAPTER TWO

LITERATURE REVIEW

2.1 Introduction:

Successful writers carefully select their words and phrases that may contain similes, metaphors ...etc. The connotations of a word are the general meanings usually ascribed to that word, which may or may not be the same as the denotation represented in the dictionary definition. Sometimes writers like to choose words that serve more than one function, or words that help deepen the reader's understanding of the intended meaning; due to the fact that connotation is a culture specific meaning and each culture has its own connotations. As far as the conceptualization of zoomorphicism is concerned, one has to make recognizable shift in connotation when s/he moves from Arabic into English. This shift is attributed to that what has negative or positive connotation in English culture is not necessarily has the same connotation in Arabic and vice versa. Meaning, on one hand, is the raw material of any communicative act among nations. On the other hand, being familiar with the cultural living customs and convention, people can communicate with English-speaking communities understandably and confidently, so that the speaker or writer will be able to convey the meaning in the best communicative channel.

2.2 The Concept of Meaning:

Meaning is the most ambiguous and most controversial theory of language. However, Lacey (1996: 196) mentions that considerations of what meanings are have mainly concerned words and sentences which differ from each other. Sentences have meanings because of the lexemes in them. Conversely, lexemes only have meaning because they are built-in to perform function in sentences. Reviewing the concept of meaning, Crystal (2003: 286) states that the meaning issue requires reference to non-linguistic factors, such as: knowledge, situation, use, intention ... etc.

Similarly, Greenberg and Harman (2005: 1) state that expressions of meaning are determined or explained by the role of the expressions in thinking. Fløistad (2005: 3) argues that any analysis of meaning should take into account both experiences and communication, in addition to the rules that constitute the use of language. Meaning somehow unifies the elements constitutive of experience: the objects, the situation and the events together with man and language. Tanesini (2007: 161) defines the theory of meaning for a language as a theory that attributes to each expression in the language its literal meaning, spelling out what is known by speakers who understand the expressions (i.e., their linguistic competence). Likewise, it is usually argued that it is unanimously agreed in Cognitive Linguistics that meaning does not only inhabit in linguistic items but rather is assembled in the minds of the language speakers. For the listener, this necessitates that s/he views linguistic units as stimuli from which an expressive conceptual demonstration will be made (Radden, et. al. 2007: 1). In this regard, it is of significance that one should make a distinction between various types of meaning. What is relevant to this study is to show the difference between connotation and denotation.

2.3 Connotative Vs. Denotative Meaning:

Abdulwahid and Ibrahim (2011: 4) refer to connotative meaning as what the sentence means when readers think about it. Whereas denotative meaning, they add, is what the sentence here means what it is about. Chandler (2002: 140) states that the term 'connotation' is used to refer to the socio-cultural and personal associations (ideological, emotional, etc.) of the sign. These are typically related to the interpreter's class, age, gender, ethnicity and so on. Signs are more 'polysemic' open to interpretation - in their connotations than their denotations. Denotation is sometimes regarded as a digital code and connotation as an analogue code (ibid). Kim (1996: 24) shows that a connotative meaning is not present in the dictionary. For example, 'home' has several connotative meanings. Connotations, then, are subjective meanings people add to signs, based on their special experiences and feelings. Depending on how a person experiences 'home', the connotative meanings may vary. To somebody, 'home' may mean 'paradise'. To others, the same home may mean 'hell'. Connotations reflect subjective values that are randomly added to a sign by an interpreter. The important point is that connotative meanings of a sign stem from the interpreter's cultural experiences with a referent represented by the sign. Making use of word connotation is very common in the area of literature, especially because ideas or situations are expressed and even subjects are presented tacitly so that the reader or interpreter of the text can easily understand meaning. For example, 'That woman is an angel'. In this case, a woman is connoted as a good, charitable person and in which a certain degree of confidence can be held. The meaning of the expression 'is an angel' cannot be taken literally, it is simply a way of expressing and exposing a characteristic of that subject. It is also very common to words or phrases with animal connotations in the day to day through the communication of people as they are used as prerogative expressions. People usually make use of a connotative language with the intention of being in high in style or more effective.

Denotation indicates a simple, unambiguous, direct relationship between a sign and its referent. For example, the denotative meaning of 'home' is 'shelter' or 'a place to live'. There is no ambiguity in denotative meaning because it is objective and concrete. Denotation occurs when a signified is known to everyone in the same manner. Hence, nobody quarrels over denotative meanings, as these meanings are so obvious. It is worth noting that denotations are a kin to dictionary meanings (ibid.: 26). Denotation is the precise anonymity of the term connotation. On the one hand, the denotation is the main meaning of the words, which can find in any dictionary or glossary (Hu & Kye, 2019: 118). Conversely, the connotation is the aggregate meaning, determined by the context. Within the denotative sense of a word, there is no room for inconsistencies. But in the case of the connotative signifier, the situation changes. Interpretations of connotation may lead to controversy, as this meaning may not be shared by one of the people based on their personal experience. Connotation and denotation are two meanings that almost every word has. If the connotation refers to the double meaning or secondary meaning that words or phrases possess according to context, then, for their part, denotation is the main or objective meaning of a word that is recognized by all people. For example, 'Ali is a lion'. If it is taken literally, then its meaning would exactly be as 'a lion is named Ali'. On the other hand, if it is taken figuratively, its meaning would be as 'Ali is as brave as a lion'. In the second case, the connotative meaning is considered not the denotative one. Also, it can can say, 'Your friendship is worth gold'. In this case, the meaning of the word gold ceases to be used in a denotative way and by context and connotation, it is understood that a friendship is being referred to that is highly appreciated and is worth much more than anything else. There are numerous examples of connotation in our everyday language. Certain uses and customs are so ingrained in our communication that are likely to use them without thinking about it. As for the images, for example, we usually interpret a table served with candles and flowers as a romantic dinner. If it were roses, it would increase that connotative meaning, since we usually associate them with love (ibid: 119).

Finally, it is of significance that to be acquainted with the so-called: cultural connotation. It refers cultural meaning approved in various cultural circumstance, it includes the meaning additional and the amplified meaning with unusual social and cultural parameters. Likewise, it includes the attitudes and emotions of some precise cultural group. translators should wisely apply the terms and phrases of ZEs whenever communicating with foreigners or doing translation. Therefore, it is a challenging task to deliver the cultural connotation of ZEs into other cultures (Cui Xuena, 2015: 58).

2.4 Types of Connotation:

Connotation can be divided into three main categories: negative, positive, and neutral, or at times both negative and positive, according to the way they are employed.

2.4.1 Negative Connotation:

It is a lexical item whose nuance involves negative feelings and associations. If one replaces the word 'fragrance' in the previously mentioned sentence it will read 'the stink of my grandma's food preparation,' the sense changes entirely. Despite the fact that both 'fragrance' and 'stink' refer to the smell, 'stink' has an unacceptable nuance; therefore, the food sounds to a great extent less likable. Similarly, the sentence which suitably fits in this regard 'the dog is emaciated' has negative connotations because the word 'emaciated' implies the dog has neglectful owner (Çepýk, 2006: 146).

2.4.2 Positive Connotation:

It is a lexical item whose nuance involves positive feelings and associations. For example, 'the fragrance of my grandma's food preparation' gives a positive associative meaning, since the lexical item "fragrance" means that the aroma is agreeable and attractive. Moreover, the sentence 'go-getter' implies that someone who is lively and curious as 'youthful' (ibid.: 145).

2.4.3 Neutral Connotation:

It is a lexical item whose nuance is not stable. It is neither negative nor positive. For instance, when we discuss a subject on a pet, the lexical item 'dog' has an unbiased nuance. While, the lexical item 'mutt' refers to something with negative nuance, and the lexeme 'purebred' refers to a positive nuance. Likewise, the example 'He is ambitious' suggests a person who works hard and strives, without judgment on whether the ambition is a good or a bad thing (ibid.:146). As far as this study is concerned, another class of connotation may be cited as below.

2.4.4 Connotation in Arabic

Connotative meaning is one of the most challenging aspects in translation, especially between two different cultures such as English and Arabic. The problem is more aggravated when the translation occurs from a certain sophisticated text such as the proverbs. As a result, losses in translation occur. This study, therefore, is an attempt to identify the losses in the translation of connotative meaning in zoomorphic expressions, propose strategies to reduce such losses, and identify the causes of such losses. The analysis of the extracted data revealed that connotative meaning was quite challenging in translation and losses occurred. These problems in preserving the connotative meaning of the source text (ST) word or playing it down are due to two main causes: the first cause is the lack of equivalence, while the second one is the translator's failure to pick the most appropriate equivalent. Non-equivalence problems were mainly represented in lack of lexicalization, semantic complexity, culturally-bound terms, difference in expressive meaning, and difference in distinction of meaning between the source language (SL) and the target language (TL). Some strategies were suggested to reduce such loss in the translation of connotative meaning. These strategies include footnoting, transliteration, periphrastic translation, and accuracy of selecting the proper equivalent that can be achieved by triangulation procedures such as peer-checking and expert-checking.

2.5 Zoomorphic Connotation:

Besides their exact meanings, words may have bad or good connotations. For example, lion and pig both mean 'animal'. However, lion has good connotations, or suggests something positive. Pig, on the other hand, has bad connotations, or suggests something negative. Animal has a negative connotation by Itself. It suggests negative feelings if it is used as such. Due to historical, social, cultural and linguistic differences each country has many popular sayings associated to animals. Malcolm (2003: 85) points out that language users understand the meanings of words in terms of the beliefs, values, expectations and stereotypes associated with their cultures. Despite the common referent thing in the world, each language has its own referring expressions: in English 'cat'; in French 'chat'. Communicators also understand the meaning of the present instantial discourse by comparing it to their non-instantial memories of past linguistic experiences of such meanings. Berko, et al. (1992: 145) say that the meaning

that we derive from our language stems from how we as communicators interpret the symbols used in that language because words do not have meanings as such, we derive our meaning from the verbal symbols through our understanding. For Baker (2003: 92), connotation involves meanings that are generated by connecting signifiers to wider cultural concerns. Here, meaning involves the association of signs with other cultural codes of meaning. Thus, 'pig' may connote nasty police officer or male chauvinist according to the sub-codes or lexicons at work.

In a nutshell, since there are cultural differences, there are many forms of implicit expressions and senses. After the connotative meaning has been explained, it is necessary to be familiar with the concept of zoomorphism.

2.6 The Concept of Zoomorphism:

According to Webster's Dictionary (1984: 13) zoomorphism means: (1) the transformation of men into beasts; (2) the quality of representing or using animal form, as zoomorphism in ornament. Osipian (2018: 64) states that zoomorphism denotes the tendency of viewing human behavior in terms of the behavior of animal contrary to anthropomorphism which views animal or nonanimal behavior in human terms. For Werness (2006: 85), zoomorphism is a kind of animal symbolism that works in two directions, anthropomorphism-projecting human qualities upon animals and zoomorphism –imagining humans as animals. Werness (ibid), believes that anthropomorphism is more common than zoomorphism and it tells us comparatively little about animals; an anthropomorphic text assumes a basic identification, such as lion as a king. Although the object of the discourse is theoretically an animal, the text imagines the animal as behaving the way human does. Zoomorphism, on the other hand, is more complex although this time a human being is the explicit object. Radhakrishna, et al. (2012: 58) see zoomorphism as a detailed observation of bestial qualities that it assigns to human beings but it is less common than anthropomorphism in pre-modern literature. Fudge (2010: 19) considers ZEs as a kind of literary satire that could take a variety of forms. In the exchange of invective or abuse, the most direct form of satire, the target might be called an animal. Rashidian (2014: 80) points out that zoomorphism is a kind of trope that compares humans to animals, and thereby implies similarity. He adds (ibid.), that zoomorphism can be seen as a kind of human animality and it might be positive or negative. Human animality for him is those basic aspects of embodiment such as physical movements and appetites. For Knutsen et al (2012: 364) ZEs are a kind of derogatory language. It is one of the most common linguistic devices used to attack and devaluate the identity and life style of the others through the use of such pejorative animal metaphor in which people are described by animal negative attributes via replacing them with human characteristics (ibid.). Todes (2014: 1) views anthropomorphism and zoomorphism as two moments of a single conceptual process in which the features of animals are given to humans on the basis of the constant conceptual interplay between experiences and understandings of animals and people. ZEs reflect the symbolic connotations evoked by certain animals and they work according to the culture and traditions of a certain language. He adds (ibid.), it is a phenomenon common to all languages and cultures to attach symbolic value to some animals that are abundant in cultural and traditional connotations. Now it is importance to be acquainted with this concept across cultures, namely, Arabic and English in our case.

2.7 Zoomorphism in Arabic and English Culture:

It is the methodology of attributing material states we know from the study of nonhuman animals to humans (Nancy, 2000: 1). Etymologically, the word zoomorphism originates from the Greek word (zoo), which means 'animal' and (morphe), meaning 'shape' or 'form' These two notions joined to produce the adjective 'zoomorphic'. Unlike anthropomorphism, which stands for animal or non-animal conduct in human terms, zoomorphism is the inclination of considering human acts given the animal's behavior. Historically speaking, it is used to depict human deeds with animalistic activities or characteristics (Werness, 2006: 23). Across cultures, zoomorphic lexeme has its denotation in addition to being cultural associate.

Clearly, the same animal words or various animal words, have similar to dissimilar cultural connotations across cultures that are conceptualized via languages. Consequently, it brings about cultural shock and misapprehension in intercultural interaction.

For Best (1958: 85-90) and Al-Askari (1988:450-1), Arabic uses the zoomorphic expression 'يأكل السبع' as a symbol of greediness and excessive eating and the expression 'أغدر من ذئب' as a simple of betrayal while English has different expressions as in the table below:

Animal	Connotation	Translation Examples
السبع /Camel or Wolf	Eating too much	يأكل السبع
ذئب /Striped hyena	Betrayal	أغدر من ذئب

Table (2-1): The Difference between English and Arabic Connotative Expressions

Further, many animal words encapsulate different connotations across cultures. For instance, in the Arabic culture the image of pessimism is stuck to 'crow'. So, it is said 'أشأم من غراب' which means 'more ominous than a crow'. In English, both 'crow' and 'monkey' refer to pessimism (Al-Maydani, 2010: 482-1; Thomas and Fogen, 2017: 429 & 431). The chart below gives further illustration.

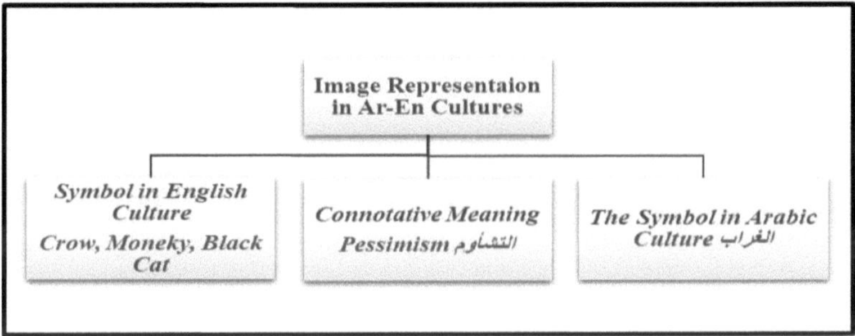

Fig. (2-1): Cross-Cultural Different Realizations of Pessimism

Languages, in general, are influenced by each other as far as culture is concerned. People, accordingly, share different opinions the same thing (Liu, 2013: 18). The cultural differences are not confined to Arabic and English, rather they extend to other. Britain and China, for example, have many of the same animals, the dragon, in the Chinese culture symbolizes power and nobility. In the west this animal signifies evil and danger (ibid.). Since animals are human's companions from time immoral, humans have observed and understood their characteristics and even domesticates some Phuong and Dung (2016: 20). The animals that human have understood is the 'snake'. In the English Culture, it is symbol of evil and danger; the same is with the Vietnamese language of these animals that have been domesticated is the dog. In English Culture it is a symbol for friendship it is man's best friend

.In the Vietnamese culture it is a symbol for stinginess and hatred. A bee, which is a black and yellow flying insect which makes honey, is a symbol of 'business' and 'hard work' in both Chinese and English. Similarly, in the English and Chinese cultures, the tiger represents 'danger', 'cruelty', and 'ferocity'(ibid.).

2.8 Zoomorphism Vs. Anthropomorphism:

Zoomorphism & anthropomorphism exist in all cultures. Astrology, for example, is riddled with zoomorphic signs: anthropomorphism, on the other hand, attributes human characteristics or human names to animals, plants, things, and places. Anthropomorphism is a word that means 'as human'. It is used to attribute human characteristics to a non-human being or object. However, the word can be applied to anything other than human, including animals, plants, and inanimate objects. Zoomorphism, on the other hand is used to describe humans with animal characteristics, with the idea that the result is still mainly human; for example, 'a human with the patience of a camel' (in Arabic culture). This meaning comes from the use of camel's image as a symbol of patience and the person compared to that animal. Vallely et al. (2012: 351) state that zoomorphism is the flip-side of anthropomorphism or the attribution of animalistic properties to people. Where anthropomorphism simply leaps over our knowledge that most animals cannot speak, zoomorphism seizes upon language as a point of potential difference between humans and animals and worries that point in various ways, imputing human speech to certain individual animals and either muteness or, on the other hand, the ability to understand animals to certain individual humans.

Werness (2006: 97) sees anthropomorphism and zoomorphism as two different attempts to reduce the otherness between humans and animals, to see the sameness beneath the difference. But sameness, just like difference, may lead to the inhuman treatment of both humans and non-humans. The ethical decision to treat animals according to the basic standards of human decency is one that must be taken regardless of whether we prefer to emphasize the qualities that they share with us – such as their instincts and drives or those that they are not their systems of communication.

2.9 Zoomorphic Allegory:

Childs & Fowler (2006: 17) define allegory as "a major symbolic mode that is often defined as an 'extended metaphor' in which characters, actions and scenery are systematically symbolic, referring to spiritual, political, psychological confrontations." In such kind of allegory, the writer or the speaker uses an animal image as a symbol or reflection of an intended meaning in his mind depending on the assumption that the receptors of the produced discourse are familiar with the underlying or associative meaning of that image. Zoomorphic allegory might be in the form of metaphor, simile, proverb or metonymy. Now, let us view each type of the allegorical forms used in this work as they are explained in the following figure:

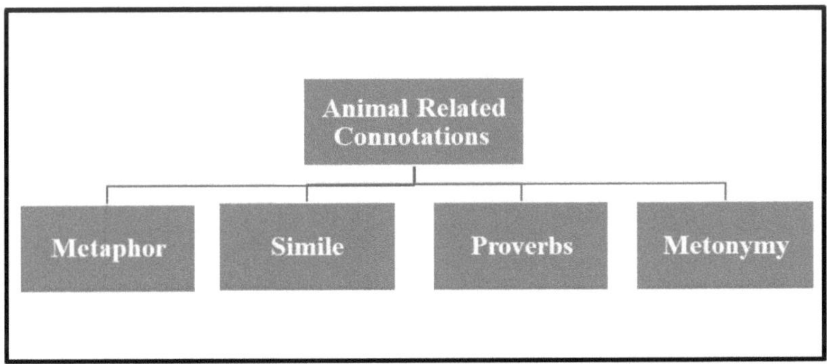

Fig. (2-2): Classification of Animal Related to Connotation Types under Study

2.9.1 Zoomorphic Metaphor:

Metaphor, is one of the cognitive and linguistic devices, involves cultural knowledge and beliefs. By means of metaphor, speakers communicate their views and attitudes towards the world around them. What makes this possible is the fact that metaphor has the feature of being laden with subjective elements that mirror speakers' feelings towards things, actions, events or other people. Animal metaphor is a good example of this, expressing people's views of other people. It has been claimed that the use of animal metaphors in language is overwhelmingly negative and goes against speakers' positive attitudes towards animals (Pagani, et al., 2014: 131). Now, Consider the following examples that show the cultural influences on the use of 'dog' and 'pig' in English and Arabic metaphors with the aim of exploring the way dog behavior is used to represent human behavior or character.

1. John becomes a pig at feast.   (*يصبح جون خنزيراً عند الولائم).
2. A good dog deserves a good bone.   (*الكلب الجيد يستحق عظمة جيدة)

In the above mentioned examples, the animal metaphor is achieved differently due to the cultural differences between English and Arabic. Accordingly, one sees the word 'pig' as a symbol of a ravenous person while in Arabic the same sense is achieved by the use of another animal image that behaves as a ravenous person 'lion'.

2.9.2 Zoomorphic Simile:

Seely and Shakespeare (2005: 235) state that simile is a type of vivid figurative language-using. It is a way of describing one thing by comparing it with another. By doing this, similes generally give a richer, more memorable description than simple adjectives can achieve. Similes are usually introduced by the words 'as' or 'like'. Animal analogy is a good way of expressing people's views of other people. The analogy might be of positive or negative meaning depending on people's choice of the animal image and its connotation in their culture. Now, consider the following examples:

3. As brave as a lion.	(شجاع كالأسد)
4. Free like a bird.	(حرٌّ كالطير)
5. As slow as a snail.	(* بطيء كالحلزون)
6. Blind like a bat.	(* أعمى كالخفاش)

Thus, the lexical items 'snail' & 'bat' in English culture must be replaced by other animal names that perform the same function in Arabic (i.e. 'bear' & 'turtle').

2.9.3 Zoomorphic Proverbs:

Proverbs are concise traditional statements of apparent truths common among people. More elaborately stated, proverbs are short, generally known sentences of the folk that contain wisdom, truths, morals, and traditional views in a metaphorical, fixed, and memorizable form and that are handed down from one generation to another. (Mieder, 1996a: 597). Animal based proverbs are other good ways of expressing people's views of other people. Animal image in this kind of figurative use of language also might be the same as the other languages or different. Consider the following examples:

7. A hog in satin is still a hog.	(* الخنزير مرتدياً الساتان يبقى خنزيراً)
8. A leopard cannot change its spots.	(* الفهد ليس بمقدوره تغيير بقع جلده)
9. The early bird catches the worm.	(* الطير الباكر يصطاد الدودة)

2.9.4 Zoomorphic Metonymy:

Littlemore (2015: 4) defines metonymy as "a figure of language and thought in which one entity is used to refer to, or in cognitive linguistic terms 'provide access to', another entity to which it is somehow related." In order to illustrate this, let us look at the following animal-related metonymy examples:

10. He left the meeting with his tail down.   (ترك الاجتماع وذيله إلى الأسفل *)

11. John stood with his rear up.   (نهض جون وعجزه إلى الأعلى *)

In order to understand these sentences, one has to use the knowledge of the real world and cognition, including the fact that human beings do not have tail, or they put their rears up in discussion. Thus, one gives the condition of an animal to a human being to show the real situation of a person via our cognitive knowledge of the real world and what such a description means. It is worth mentioning here that culture plays a vital role in deciding the type of the image to be used in TL.

The coming sections are allocated for translating ZEs. However, it is necessary to give a general introduction about translation beforehand.

2.9.5 Zoomorphic Expressions in Arabic

Arabic provides countless examples of zoomorphism in animals and as these objects come from an Arabic heritage, they are often removed from context due to the tradition, people, or animals. Therefore, most animal figurative representation in Arabic comes from animals. The zoomorphic style allows to stylize animal forms and designs, a tradition that has been present as early as the seventh century after the spread of Islam beyond the Arabian Peninsula.

One example of a zoomorphic object is the incense burner of Amir Saif Al-Dunya wa'l-Din ibn Muhammad Al-Mawardi, today located at the Metropolitan Museum in New York. Incense burners were common objects for zoomorphic forms that served as a container for aromatic material to be burned. This particular object comes from the Seljuq period in Iran. It is made of bronze, meaning it was a more expensive object as metalwork incense burners cost more to produce and were less common than other productions made of clay or soft stones. The work is meant to depict a lion or large cat. The artist plays with the anatomical elements of the body to fit the use for burning incense. Around the base of neck shows the area where the head is designed to be removed for the insertion of coal and incense. Throughout the body small holes were punctured for the release of the smoke. This object would have been found in a domestic space due to the animal-like imagery.

Another example of zoomorphism in Islamic art is the bird-shaped oil lamp, located at the Metropolitan Museum of Art in New York. The oil lamp would have been used as an everyday object in a domestic space as well. The handle of the lamp is depicted by the head and neck of the bird. The body takes the form of the base of the lamp where oil can be poured in the small opening. The artist uses the form of the bird to utilize the lamp either hanging or resting. There are keyholes on either side of the body for the lamp to be hung by a chain and the flat base allows for the lamp to be placed on any smooth surface. The similarities between the incense burner and the lamp demonstrate how zoomorphism was used throughout Islamic culture.

Zoomorphism appears on objects beyond household items. An example of this is the Dagger with Zoomorphic Hilt also located at the Metropolitan Museum of Art in New York. The hilt or handle of the dagger merges into the shape of a dragon attacking a lion who is performing the same act onto a deer. Each attacking animal is connected by its claws and teeth to form the handle. The inclusion of Persian and Indian symbols of power was common in zoomorphic imagery on hilts of daggers. [In this dagger there is a figure of a bird in front of the deer who is meant to represent the Indian deity Garuda. Due to the intricate design and craftsmanship of this dagger, it would most likely not have been used for the purposes of a weapon, but rather as a ceremonial object. Many of the weapons included in Islamic art served as symbols for power and wealth.

2.10 Translation Definition:

If one takes into account all the elements involved in the translation process, he/she will find different definitions of the term that respond, in short, to different points of view, the following definitions might make the notion of translation clear:

For Catford (1965: 39), translation is "The substitution of textual material in one language (SL) by equivalent textual material in another language (TL)". Nida and Taber (2003: 28) argue that "Translation consists in reproducing, through a natural and exact equivalence, the message of the original language in the receiving language, first in terms of meaning and then in terms of style." Newmark (1988: 28) considers that translating "Many times, though not always, is to pour into another language the meaning of a text in the sense intended by the author." Toury (1995: 26) states that "Translation in the strict sense is the replacement of one message, encoded in one natural language, by an equivalent message, encoded in another language." Hurtado (2001: 40) says that translation is "an act of communication, an operation between texts (and not between languages) and a mental process." It is "a communicative process that takes place in a social context" (Hatim & Mason, 1990: 13).

For (Seleskovitch & Lederer, 1984: 256), translating means conveying the meaning of the messages contained in a text and not converting into another language the language in which it is formulated. House (1977: 29), mentions that "translation is an act of communication and not linguistics; the substitution of a text in the language of the heading with a semantic and pragmatically equivalent text in the target language."

And finally, let's look at Steiner's (1975: 44) opinion of translation "The schematic model of translation is that of a message from a source language that passes through a receiving language, after having undergone a process of transformation."

2.11 Translation in Terms of (SL or TL Orientation):

Today, translation is studied as a general concept covering two aspects: process and product. As a process, the translator does a dual function: a reader and a writer. As a reader s/he should analyze the text in all its dimensions; in her/his role as a writer, s/he reproduces the text in another language and for others readers. As a product, the various types of translations required for different purposes. Precisely, with regard to translation as a product, it is essential to find in popular use the inaccurate classification of a translation as 'faithful', 'literal', or 'wrong', without it being taken into account what a literal translation is, what makes it faithful, or why it is inaccurate. Just as to make it, to judge a translation it is necessary to keep in mind many factors: the intention, the purpose and type, the style, the readers, the quality, the place and form of publication (magazine, book, advertisement), both of the original and the translated version. The reason is obvious: for example, what might be correct for the translation of a scientific text would not be for a literary one.

Therefore, explains the need to precisely delimit the different types of translation. Newmark (1988: 46), for example, has systematized several types of Translation in a range ranging from "word-by-word translation" that emphasizes the original language and text, at one end, to "adaptation", which emphasizes terminal language and text, at the other hand. Starting with those that tend more towards the original language or text, even to the loss of understanding in the target language, like: word-by-word translation, literal translation, faithful, semantic translation; and, on the other side, communicative translation, free translation and, finally, adaptation, which more respect the conventions of the target language and culture. Translation in terms of SL or TL orientation can be represented by the following figure:

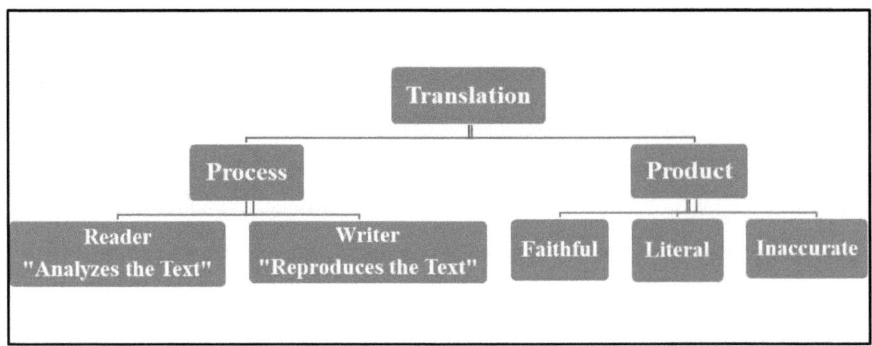

Fig. (2-3): Translation in Terms of SL and TL Orientation Suggested by (Nida, 1964: 79)

The process of translation begins with investigating the SL text. Here, the linguistic competence of a translator that helps him to properly understand and recognize the SL is extremely needed. Our understanding of the subject substance will assist our task at this step. Among the difficulties that a translator may face at this early stage is possibly lack of intelligibility of the source language text and the problem of untranslatability (Nolan, 2005: 57).

Absence of intelligibility in the source language text might be in unrevised texts. Thus, a translator needs to toil harder in understanding and analyzing the sense of the SL to recognize what precisely the intent of the original writer is. If essential, a translator might resort to the writer to look for explanation (ibid.:58).

The next step in the process of translation is transference. The message is transferred into the TL. In this step, a translator can make use of a dictionary, lexicon, and other applicable supportive resources. The capability to select the suitable correspondent in the target language text is a necessity to guarantee that the meaning is properly offered in the target language text among the difficulties that a translator might encounter at this step is absence of counterparts in the target language text, for instance, translating a manuscript from Arabic into English, a translator might find it problematic to find a correspondent item in the target language text for a specific cultural item (Plotkin, 2006:11).

As Arabic is better-off in terms compared to the English language, we might find it difficult to find counterparts in English. In such case, a translator can make use of extra words to compensate the sense elements not conveyed by a word in the other language. There are some translation methods that can be used by a translator according to the context, the TL audience and the sort of the text (ibid.:12).

Step no.3 is restructuring. Since each language has a unique structural system, transposition in translation is inevitable. It is tolerable if the sense of ST message is properly offered in the target language. This step can also be viewed as a revising step that comprises decision making. At this step a translator needs to appropriately adopt an equivalent and strategy. A translator here, needs to decide whether to make his rendition faithful as in translating law documents or to make a dynamic rendition as in rendering a literary text. A translator has to be mindful of the indirect meaning of the text and diminish the amounts of grammatical errors in the target language text. As for example, in translating Arabic text into English, a translator must know the exact use of tenses, and the parts of speech (ibid.:17). This can be represented in the following figure:

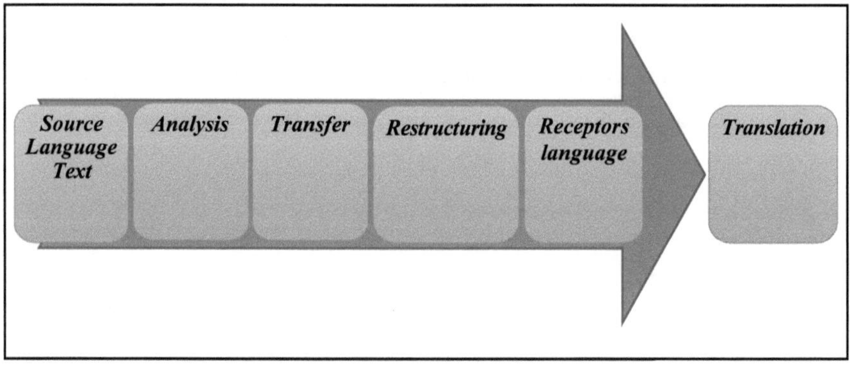

Fig. (2-4): The Model Proposed by Nida for Translation Process Suggested by (Nida, 1964: 105)

To put it briefly, problems must not stop us from taking on a tricky translation task. We must understand that difficulties are for all time there in any aspect. Consequently, rather than considering them as hurdles or problems, we can consider them as tests to our ability and deal with them confidently to encourage ourselves to repeatedly gain knowledge and improve our value, and lastly attempt to be professionals in our specialization. Since most ZEs are culturally shaped, it is of significance here to allude to those aspect of cultural problematic areas of which the ZEs are a part.

2.12 Cultural Problems in Translation:

Culture is commonly related to real knowledge which usually includes political institutions, education, history, current affairs, religion, and customs. The question of how to abide by cultural criteria is itself a dilemma for the translator. Newmark (1991: 8) indicates that the words encoding cultural information are difficult to be translated since they involve cultural and background knowledge. Ezzat (1993: 51) points out that the cultural equivalence is delusional because it is difficult to find absolute meanings within the same culture. He also suggests two possibilities forgetting over cultural problems in translation, using footnotes and glosses that explain the relevant traits of the situation in which the cultural term takes place in question (ibid).

Aziz and Lataiwish (2000: 90) note that many problematic areas will appear due to the fact that the cross-cultural translation results from differences in the origin of the two languages (e.g. English and Arabic). According to Nida (2001: 21), it is not easy to fulfill a successful transfer because cultural differences between two languages are definitely found. Furthermore, it is difficult to transfer the meaning of dependent words in another language, especially when they are connected to cultural domains.

Ghazala (2002: 21) sees that, occasionally, Islamic terms lead to differences in culture when superficially translated and many Islamic terms have no equivalence in the target language culture. Such an absence of the equivalence will leave the translator in a lurch. Moreover, culture-bound terms limit the translator in a narrow space and s/he, therefore, should solve the problem of rendering them by using footnotes, but without overuse.

Al-Jabri (2006: 33) hypothesizes that the major impediment to rendering religious terms is not only due to the difference in culture, images, and conceptions, but also to the cultural burdens that are not explicitly observed in the ST.

Many problems arise because of cross-cultural differences in translation. Hence, the kinds of cultural problems in rendition are linguistic ones, including those related to idioms, proverbs, and metaphor, ecology, geography, society, material, religion, …etc. Newmark (1988: 95) classifies culture into five various categories and presents illustrative examples for each:

1. Ecological Culture: it includes plants of certain area, animals, local winds, plains, mountains, and hills among others. In this respect, the names of 'snow', 'camel', 'sward' … etc.
2. Material culture: it involves such notions as food, clothes, houses and towns, transport and communication, … etc. Such examples are 'عِقال' and 'kimono'.
3. Social culture: it refers to work and leisure. This can be exemplified by 'patisserie' (حلويات) and 'chapellerie' (متجر القبعات).
4. Political and administrative, religious, and artistic aspects: all are related to the category of organizations, activities, customs, and ideas indicating the institutional terms which mirror the political and social life of a country; for example, 'Riksdag' (i.e. 'برلمان' in some states like France and Sweden).
5. Gestures and habits: they refer to the way people of different cultures behave differently in specific situations, as is the case with 'greeting' or 'kissing'.

2.12.1 Ecological Cultural Problems:

According to Nida (1964: 91), he denotes that it is difficult for the translator to find the equivalent due to ecological variation from one region to another. Moreover, the geographical elements are regarded as a part of certain culture. Hence, it can be said that one of the main difficulties in translation is the ecological cultural problems; since the translator may face various meanings in his/her target cultural words versus the source cultural ones due to the fact relating to different ecological environments. That is, meaning of a word is determined and influenced by ecological culture and the same word in both cultures may have different meanings. Accordingly, the translator should be familiar with the connotations of words across cultures so that he/she can be in a safe side during the process of translation.

In this respect, Aziz (1982: 26) suggests that Arabic is affected by Arab land climate, notably the hotness and dryness. Likewise, English is affected by British Isles climate, especially the coldness and wetness. In other words, vocabulary of both languages are undoubtedly influenced by the climatic condition. Consider the following example:

12. The news warmed my heart.   (الأخبار أثلجت صدري).

13. Warm-hearted man.   (رجل طيب).

(Ilyas, 1989: 128)

In this regard, it is worthy to shed light on another problem related to ecological culture; that is the 'phatic communion'. According to Palmer (1976: 40), its main function is establishing and maintaining feelings of community solidarity and it is not used for offering information or to convey meaning. Newmark (1982: 169) mentions that 'phatic communion' comprises phrases of greeting and small talks, and their expressions are different from one community to another. For instance, conversations about the weather in English community serve as the subject-matter for phatic stereotyped, due to the fact that such a weather is so fickle or temperate.

41

Hence, the translator has to differentiate the phatic form from the denotative element and he/she must render it in a way that is in harmony with the TL equivalent taking this particular point into consideration. In other words, the translator cannot render the phatic expression literally due to the fact that such an expression will keep its literal meaning and, consequently, he/she substitute the SL expression by the TL one which serves the social function between the conversation parts. For instance, we can substitute the English expression "It is a nice weather this morning, right?" by the appropriate function behind such an expression like "صباح الخير" in Arabic. that is, the social function of such an expression is for greeting a friend early in the morning. By the same token, the translator may replace the Arabic expression 'السلام عليكم' by the English one 'it's another nice day' which is used to open utterance between a seller and a buyer, for instance, since both of them comprise the same function.

Connectedly, local names or words may highly enrich the text, especially with they are required to be introduced in the TT due to their appropriateness in describing a site or a landscape. Yet, if they do not have an extremely influence to the text, in this case the translator may tend to render the message only. Consider the example below:

14. Tundra.   (سهل قطبي أجرد).

Hence, Newmark (2001: 95-101) does agree with Nida in his attitude saying that certain ecological elements are strange or unknown to the culture, and they may be regarded as untranslatability cases in the process of translation.

2.12.2 Material Cultural Problems:

It is to be noted that physical reality can be viewed in each language in a different way. Agha (2001: 2-3) suggest that such a difference in way of languages segment external reality is natively approved by the notion that a specific language may have more subdivisions than others in certain semantic fields.

Making a survey on each language, especially when a society concentrates on a specific subject matter, increases numerous words to distinguish its unique language or lexicology. For example, the German concentrate on sausages, the French on wines and types of cheese, the English on sports, the Arab on camels, … etc. So, different languages, for instance, may also have different kinds of clothes and food. That is, national costumes are considered, translator can face names of clothes and food, then he/she may tend to make a transliteration for such words, e.g. 'جبة', 'عمامة', 'kimono', 'jeans', 'sari', and many others. The same case is with the kinds of food, like 'sushi', 'دولمة', 'macaroni'….etc. Here, it can be stated that the reasons behind adopting the transliteration procedure by the translator is due to the fact that there is no equivalent for such cultural terms. Thus, such words will be loaned from one language into another (ibid).

According to Lyons (1981: 310), there are certain things that can't be said at all in particular languages, simply because the vocabulary with which to say them does not exist.

Newmark (2001: 97) mentions that the translator may face some problems during the process of rendering some material culture aspects like food, since it can be done by transference if there is no recognized equivalent. For example, the SL word 'sushi' can be only rendered by transference into Arabic because it doesn't exist in the TL culture and it hasn't a specific equivalent. So, it will be 'سوشي' in Arabic.

By the same token, technological development was the main reason behind spawning a plethora of words like 'Facebook', 'WhatsApp',

'Twitter', …etc. which have no equivalents in Arabic. On this basis, it can be stated that different languages have different referring terms, like the Italic word 'palazzo' (i.e. 'بالازو' or 'منزل كبير' in Arabic), the Swiss word 'chalet' (i.e. 'شاليه' or 'بيت صغير من الخشب على ساحل البحر' in Arabic), the Spanish word 'bungalow' (i.e. 'بنغل' or 'نوع من الأكواخ' in Arabic) (Aziz and Lataiwish, 2000: 95).

2.12. 3 Social Cultural Problems:

Not all the behaviors are common among all people, since some of them are acceptable in a specific culture but unacceptable in others and vice versa. During the process of translation, the translator will feel of that matter obviously. The social and cultural features of the SL may not be familiar to the TL reader and may also cause misunderstanding and confusion of the ST intentionality. On this basis, it can be found that the social culture evokes remarkable problems in this respect. Some of the aspects of these problems may be represented by the relationships among people like the notions toward love, marriage, and decency (Brislin, 1976: 34).

Aziz (1982: 27) argues that there are numerous differences of social cultures like kinship, social institutions, rules for behavior (i.e. etiquettes of eating, drinking, wearing, and talking) and many others. In other words, it is noted in the Arab culture that there are three meals a day (i.e. meals served at morning, mid-day, and evening). Contrasting with English culture, only breakfast can be common among Arab and English cultures.

In addition to that, the most important organizations are social conventions and institutions which keep on maintaining the aspects of culture in a certain community. According to Al-Sulaiman (2011: 84), the translator has to distinguish between the denotative and connotative meanings of the items or words via taking into consideration the 'social culture' of SL and its resulted problems by contrast with TL's. By the same token, Agha (1994: 294) argues that the social culture has the power to determine the ways of using honorifics aspects in all communities that are governed by social status of individuals.

2.13 Translation & Zoomorphic Connotation:

Establishing a cross cultural communication via the use of zoomorphic expressions supposes an even higher level of complexity because such texts are developed in a complex figurative and symbolic way. Thus, the way of communicating a message from one cultural system to another whose final recipient is the target reader must well have organized to lend a hand to the TL audience in understanding the message being communicated. Animals connote different meanings in different cultures and languages. They, therefore, refer to values and understandings which may be different from one language to another and they may arouse associations of different ideas. In Arabic, for example, many animal names are used in different sayings and different contexts. The same name of an animal may have very different connotations in a different culture while to a great extent all cultures share the same denotative of all animals (Ashley, 2009: 52). An awl in the Arabic culture, for instance, is a symbol of bad omen or bad luck. This meaning does not depend on the description of that animal but rather it is culturally handed from one generation to another and based on experience. Thus, we can say that denotative meaning is universal to some extent while connotative meaning is very specific. People usually use language in their everyday life with animal characteristics to express their attitudes towards the others. In Arabic as well as in English animals are used in allegorical forms and if one does not know the culture of the target language as well as his own culture, he will be unable to understand parabolic sense and decode the intended meaning. Sometimes a translator incorrectly keeps the image used in SL in TL as overlooking the fact that every language has its own connotations that belong to animals. Consequently, the resultant translation becomes fuzzy and unacceptable by TL audience (Al-Sulaiman, 2011: 115).

Finally, it is important to add that ZEs that are expression heavily laden with cultural associations can sometimes be transferred directly to TL and sometimes they should go through a fine cultural filtering before be transmitted to the TL audience.

2.13.1 The Adopted Model:

Usually, it is argued that translation is recommended to be target language-oriented or source language-oriented. Here comes the impact of domestication and foreignization on the translation process. In western countries, these two strategies date back to the distinction made by Horace and Cicero between sense for sense and word for word translation (Bassnett, 2004:115). Therefore, to understand 'domestication', we shall go to the adaptation definition in "Routledge Encyclopedia of Translation Studies": "Adaptation may be understood as a set of translating operations which result in a text that is recognized as representing a source text of about the same length" (Baker, 2003: 223).

It is worth mentioning that "seventeenth and eighteenth centuries were the golden age of adaptation" and "free translations during this period were defensible in terms of the need for foreign texts to be adapted to the perceptions and customs of the target culture, irrespective of the damage done to the original" (ibid.). To put it differently, domestication can be assumed as a translation strategy that formulates source text (ST) modified to the culture of the target language (TL). Therefore, cultural specific items might be getting through in the target text (TT) to substitute those of the ST. Hence the TT is easy for the target readers to understand. Therefore, domestication is actually targeted language or reader-oriented. Domestication and foreignization can be viewed as a natural extension of literal and free translation. However, domestication and foreignization first mentioned in Venuti's The Translator's Invisibility in 1995 as "A term used by Venuti to refer to the kind of translation in that a TT is created which purposely time-outs target covenants by retaining the foreignness of the original" (Shuttleworth and Cowie, 2004: 117).

Let's consider the following examples:

'white as snow' which Nida suggests to translate into *'white as egret feathers' or 'white as fungus'* can be exemplified as domestication, for 'snow', which serves as the image representing 'white', is adapted to the target culture with different images Nida and Taber, (2003: 111). In other words, to adopt domestication or foreignization in the process of translation is truly coupled with the translation strategy which determines whether the output of translation is source language-oriented or target language-oriented. Venuti in the book entitled: "The Translator's Invisibility", cites the well-known claim about translation methods: "There are only two. Either the translator leaves the author in peace, as much as possible, and moves the reader towards him; or he leaves the reader in peace, as much as possible, and moves the author towards him" (Venuti, 2004: 85). Therefore, the first is the domestication strategy and the second is the foreignization strategy. So both perform as strategies to decode and convey the original information in a proper way for the target language. Thus, domestication and foreignization

can be considered as a range in the translation process with the first on one end and the second on the other see the figure below.

Domestication ……………………..…… Foreignization

(TL Oriented)   **(SL Oriented)**

Fig. (2-5) Domestication and Foreignization Scale

It is emphasized here that in the midpoint of the scale is the shared area between domestication and foreignization. When some new items, familiarized into another language, this case may be rendered in either way. For instance, "UFO" can be translated either way of domestication or foreignization (Venuti, 2004: 89). It seems that this strategy best fits our data of the study, therefore it is best nominated as a model of the study.

2.13.2 Parameters of Domestication and Foreignization:

As is previously stated, the two strategies can be used to illustrate the source information in a subtle manner in the TL. Thus determining whether to keep the source image or apply that of the TL. instead of the source one in the course of translation, both domestication and foreignization are taken in to account (Rasul, 2019:65). In other words, deciding on translation between the dominance of the SL. or the TL. brings about the issue of domestication and foreignization. In the course of translation, there are some operators affecting the choice of the two strategies, for instance the reason to translate, text typology, the expected readers, what is preferred by the translator, and others. For instance, if the reason to translate is to introduce the foreign culture foreignization can be a better choice than domestication, and when the purpose is merely exchanging information, then domestication is much better and so the translation is smoother to grasp (ibid). The issue here is that various translators have various preference to these two strategies so different representative of the two have emerged. It can be concluded that there are no apparent criteria for the two strategies to follow or adopt. One can conclude that using either the first or the second strategy is to serve the principle of informational accessibility of the rendered texts to the TL readers. Thus the parameters that decide the choice of D or F must be built according to this principle. Within the informational accessibility as the main principle, four parameters can be distinguished determining whether to adopt D. or F. cultural acceptability of situational concept, scheme acceptability, and semantic gap (Bassnett, 2004:47). Culture and language are interrelated. language and culture are part and parcel of each other. The two are very much related to each other. That is why the power of cultural acceptability is one parameter to decide the use of either D. or F. If the image of a certain expression in the SL. is acceptable in the TL F is adopted, otherwise D is applied. Acceptability of situational context means that the factors of situational event, participants and time and space. F is adopted when the SL. meaning is accessible in the situational context, otherwise one should apply D. As for schematic acceptability, one can say that the group of people speaking various languages adopt various schemas to show the same thing. Thus some schemes or symbols used in a language can never be grasped schematically in another. So, the degree of schematic accessibility determines whether to apply F or D. If the SL. Schema is acceptable we use F or else, we use D. Finally, there is the sematic gap parameter. At times, the same expression is applied in the SL. & TL. thus there emerges the semantic gap, here D is used (ibid).

CHAPTER THREE

DATA ANALYSIS AND DISCUSSION

A test of fifteen sentences that consist of different Arabic zoomorphic expressions was distributed to (8) MA. students to be translated into English as the data of the study. The subjects are from Translation Department - College of Arts at the University of Mosul for the academic year 2019-2020. The symbols and images in the fifteen sentences are derived from three genre of figurative usage, which are 'metonymy', 'metaphor', and 'simile'. The study is mainly concerned with delving into the socio-cultural aspects that affect the process of translation. Similarly, it highlights those areas in which the cultural gap lies. Comprehensive tables are designed to perform the discussion required. The tables contain some items like: SL ZE, Subjects No., Sub.R ZE, Embedded image, Arabic-English connotation consideration, and strategies adopted by the subjects. Some analytical symbols are also used like: = that refers to recurrent analytical component, + refers to positive result, and – negative result. Then subjects' renderings are then analyzed and assessed in the light of the adopted modal, namely, Foreignization/ Domestication.

<u>ST (1)</u>:

- رأيت سبعاً يتناول العشاء في المطعم.

<u>**Subjects:**</u>

1. I saw a <u>brave man,</u> having his dinner at the restaurant.
2. I saw a <u>ravenous man,</u> having his dinner at the restaurant.
3. I saw a <u>brave man</u> having his meal at the restaurant.

4. I saw <u>strong man</u>, having his dinner at the restaurant.

5. I saw a <u>brave man</u> having his dinner at the restaurant.

6. I saw a brave <u>man (hero)</u> eating his dinner at the restaurant.

7. I saw an <u>insatiable person</u> having his dish at the restaurant.

8. I saw a <u>Greedy man</u> having his meal at the restaurant.

SL ZE	سبعأ		
Embedded Image	To express the sense of gluttony		
Sub. No.	Sub. Rs	Arabic-English connotation	The Strategy Adopted
1	Brave man	_	Domestication
2	Ravenous man	+	Domestication
3	Brave man	_	Domestication
4	Strong man	_	Domestication
5	Brave man	_	Domestication
6	Brave man (hero)	_	Domestication
7	Insatiable person	+	Domestication
8	Greedy man	+	Domestication

Table (3-1): Comprehensive Analytical Table of Subjects' Translations

Discussion:

According to Al-Askari (1988 :500\11), the Arabic (ZE) mentioned in this example refers to gluttony in eating and it is very common image in Arabic culture. However, in English this image is realized with another (ZE) that can do the same function to create the same effect on the TL readers. See the following example: "as hungry as a wolf or a camel" represents "simile" in English (Best, 1958: 88). This can be represented in the following figure:

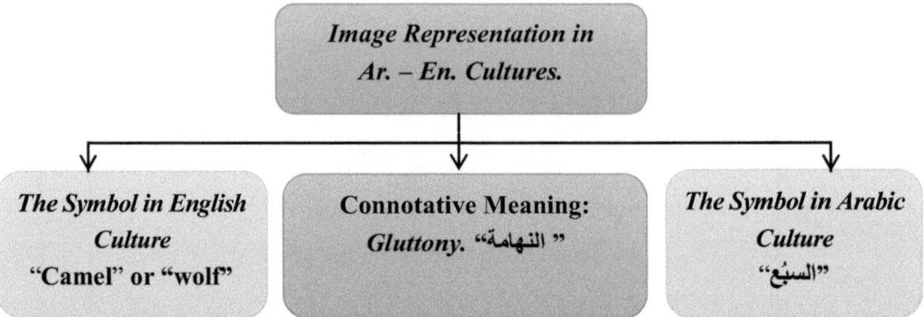

Fig. (3-1): Gluttony Representation in Ar. and En. Cultures.

sujbects no. (1, 3, 4, 5, and 6), provided inappropriate renderings of the Arabic (ZE) because they could not grasp the intended meaning of the ST (ZE). Consequently, they provided foreign images and direct similes. As for Subjects no. (2, 7, and 8), they haven't succeeded in conveying the intended meaning of the original text and they could not bring an equivalent (ZE) that is used for the same purpose in English culture and thus they failed to convey the allegorical use of language as the case in the Arabic example. A better translation might be achieved via domestication and foreignization dichotomy as illustrated below:

The Proposed Rendering:

- I saw a person having his meal at the restaurant <u>as voracious as a camel</u>.

ST (2):

- كيف يمكنك السير لمسافة طويلة كهذه دون أن تشرب الماء، أنك فعلا <u>سفينة الصحراء.</u>

Subjects:

1. How can you walk for a long distance like this without drinking water,<u> you are a real camel</u>!
2. How can you walk for a long distance such as this without drinking water, you<u> are really a tough man?</u>

3. How can you walk for a long distance like this, <u>you are a camel</u>?
4. How could you walk without drinking water, <u>you are really like a camel</u>.
5. How can you walk for a long distance without drinking water, <u>you are really a ship of desert</u>?
6. How can you travel such a long distance without water, <u>you are really a horse</u>?
7. How can you walk so much without drinking water? <u>Frankly, you are like a camel</u>.
8. How can you run such a long distance without drinking water, <u>you are like a ship of desert</u>?

SL ZE	سفينة الصحراء		
Embedded Image	To show the extent of endurance		
Sub. No.	Sub. Rs	Arabic-English connotation	The strategy adopted
1	Camel	_	Foreignization
2	Tough man	+	Domestication
3	Camel	_	Foreignization
4	Camel	_	Foreignization
5	Ship of desert	_	Foreignization
6	Horse	+	Domestication
7	Camel	_	Foreignization
8	Ship of desert	+	Foreignization

Table (3-2): Comprehensive Analytical Table of Subjects' Translations

Discussion:

Considering the camel's functions and its relationship to the desert, it can be stated that camels are symbols denoting humbleness, willingness and stubbornness in medieval art. Camels are trained to kneel down to receive heavy loads. In east, however, camels are famous as being unpleasant and obstinate .For Egyptians, Camels are symbol of objectors and those who are sluggish in their walking. (Omeysh and Malkishi, 2015: 67).

According to Ibrahim (2013: 71) in the Arabic (ZE) 'camel' is a symbol for patience, thirst, hunger and heat endurance. Thus, it has long been used metaphorically in Arabic culture to signify those who endure thirst for long periods under the stress of bearing heavy things. The image of patience is realized in English culture relying on the ZE with the 'ox' (Ferguson, 1961: 22). Despite its frequent use by the Arabs of patience image, one should not impose it into English culture because every culture has its own fauna terms and the translator has to select the appropriate term that best serves the same function in the TL.

This can be shown in the following figure:

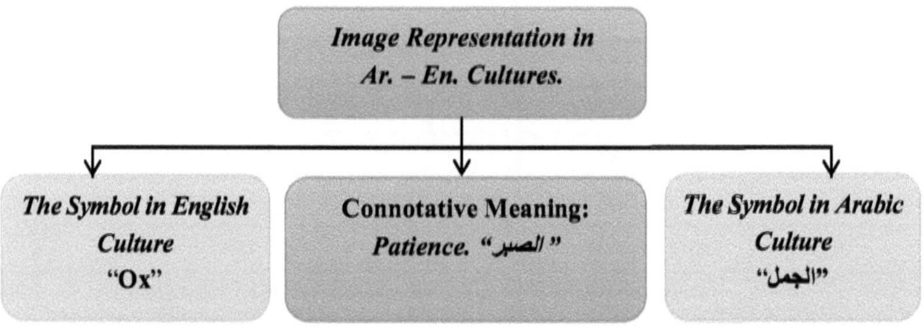

Fig. (3-2): Patience Representation in Ar. and En. Cultures.

Reviewing the translations mentioned above, we found that Subjects no. (1, 3, 4 and 7), have used 'camel' and foreignized the same image, namely 'camel', which has been directly transferred into TL without any consideration of TL cultural peculiarities and the connotative use of the word. As for Subjects no. (2, 5, and 8), they have used (*tough man, horse and ship of distance, or desert respectively*). By resorting to these metaphorical expressions, they failed to give an equivalent that suits the best function in English culture. They have manipulated the ST so as to create some effect on the TL readers. Furthermore, the expression *(distance)* is recommended to be replaced by the word *(desert)* because it has special connotations connected with (heat, soft sands, drought, coldness, and lack of vegetation). As for subject no. (6), who used *'horse'*, he/she also failed to create the intended image because *'horse'* in English culture has connotation other than patience like power, strength, nobility and courage (see the discussion of text no.7). Here, it is suggested to domesticate the SL image by bringing an equivalent image suits the culture of the TL readers with the same effect of that of SLT. One can propose the following rendering:

<u>The Proposed Rendering</u>:

- ……….. You are really <u>as patient as an ox</u>.

<u>ST (3)</u>:

- <u>قنافذ الليل</u> منبوذة من الجميع ولا يحبها أحد.

<u>Subjects:</u>

1. <u>Gossipers</u> are hateful people.

2. <u>Night snipers</u> are discarded by all and no one loves them.

3. <u>Stirrer persons are</u> not liked by anyone.

4. Nobody loves <u>Calumniators</u> and they are detested by everyone.

5. No one likes <u>Night urchins</u>.

6. Nobody likes <u>Big mouths</u>.

7. <u>Night animals</u> are most hateful for everyone.

8. <u>Night urchins</u> are forsaken, and no loves them.

SL ZE	<u>قنافذ الليل</u>		
Embedded Image	Reporting bad news about other people		
Sub. No.	Sub. Rs	Arabic-English connotation	The Strategy Adopted
1	Gossipers	+	Domestication
2	Night snipers	−	Domestication
3	Stirrer person	+	Domestication
4	Calumniators	−	Domestication
5	Night urchins	−	Foreignization
6	Big mouths	+	Domestication
7	Night animals	−	Foreignization
8	Night urchins	+	Foreignization

Table (3-3): Comprehensive Analytical Table of Subjects' Translations

<u>**Discussion:**</u>

According to Al-Askari (1988: 128) and Ibn ManZoor (2009: 617), Arabic culture uses the (ZE) 'قنفذ الليل' to refer to stirrer people because of their malice and unrest at night. A 'hedgehog' does not sleep at night, as it is the case with a stirrer person. According to *'The Big Dictionary of Dreams'*, in English this image is realized by another animal that is the *'Blackbird'* (Clarke, 2013: 272). This causes the cultural gap between the two languages. The figure below shows the image realization in both cultures:

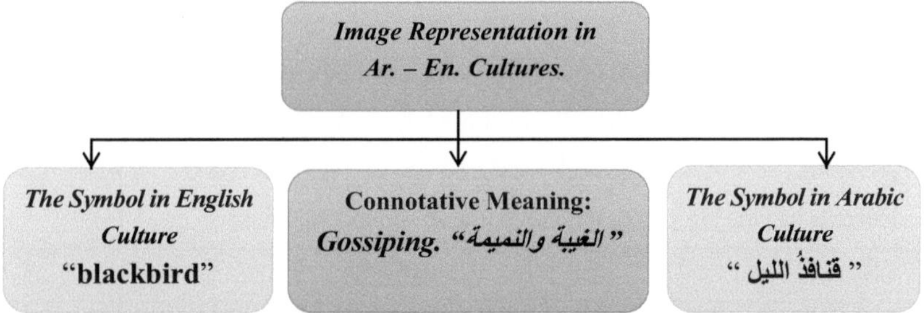

Fig. (3-3): Gossiping Representation in Ar. and En. Cultures.

After reviewing the above mentioned Subjects, one can notice that Subjects no. (1 and 3) provide the semantic content of SL (ZE). They failed in giving the (ZE) that expresses the intended image in the TT. As for Subjects no. (2, 4, and 6), they were inappropriate since they used metaphorical analogy. As for Subjects no. (5, 7, and 8), they failed to capture the intended image because they used metaphorical simile. They were also lacking the (ZE) (i.e. what is called 'zero zoomorphic expression'). This is not related to the meaning of SL, yet it is recommended here to make for the cultural gap that exists due to zero equivalence between both languages under discussion. By so doing, the translator may resort to domestication procedure that makes the TL readers more familiar with TL image.

<u>**The Proposed Rendering:**</u>

- No one likes <u>blackbird</u>.

<u>ST (4):</u>

- ‫يبدو أن أبا الاخبار لم تحمله جناحيه إلينا اليوم فبتنا لا نعلم بما يدور حولنا.‬

<u>Subjects:</u>

1. It seems that the <u>father of news</u> was unable to visit us today so we ignore what is going on.

2. <u>The news father</u> didn't inform us about the tiding news today.

3. <u>He</u> did not come today so we do not know the new news.

4. <u>The reporter</u> hasn't informed us anything.

5. It seems that the <u>talkative person</u> hasn't brought any news to us today; so we have no news.

6. The <u>hoopoe</u> hasn't come to us today, so we know nothing of what is going on.

7. It seems that our <u>news teller</u> has not come to us today. So we don't know what is going on.

8. It seems that the <u>big mouth</u> will not come so we know nothing.

SL ZE	‫أبا الأخبار‬		
Embedded Image	To express the capacity of News reporting.		
Sub. No.	Sub. Rs	Arabic-English connotation	The Strategy Adopted
1	Father of news	–	Foreignization
2	The news father	–	Foreignization
3	He	–	Foreignization
4	The reporter	+	Domestication
5	Talkative person	–	Domestication
6	Hoopoe	+	Foreignization
7	News teller	+	Domestication
8	Big mouth	–	Domestication

Table (3-4): Comprehensive Analytical Table of Subjects' Translations

<u>**Discussion:**</u>

As a nickname 'أبا الأخبار' (lit. Ab-ul- Akhbar) is attached to 'hoopoe' since it is the bird that used to report news. Furthermore, it is mentioned in the Glorious Quran (Ant chapter, verse: 23) in many exegesis books in Solomon story with hoopoe (Al-Qadhi, 2020 :64). What concerns our study in this regards is that a hoopoe in the Arabic culture usually signifies a news reporter. In the Dictionary named *"1001 idioms to master your English"* it has been stated that unfortunately in English culture the image of news reporting is realized by another bird other than 'hoopoe'. It is replaced by little bird (Skilja, 2013 :42). Let's consider the following figure:

Fig. (3-4): News Reporting Representation in Ar. and En. Cultures.

Reviewing the translations of the subjects, one can see that Subjects no. (1, & 3), have translated the ZE with formal equivalence which doesn't go with English culture. While translations no. (2, 4, & 7), were inappropriate since the subjects used metaphorical analogy. As for translations no. (5, & 8), they were inappropriate because the subjects used metaphorical simile also this has nothing to do with the meaning of the SL. Finally, the translation no. (6), although he used the word 'hoopoe', but unfortunately, it doesn't sand for the image of news reporting. The best way of rendering this image is to domesticate the symbol opting for the image that exists in the TL as mentioned above.

<u>**The Proposed Rendering:**</u>

- <u>The little bird</u> seems that it doesn't have come about. So we don't know the news.

<u>ST (5):</u>

- العدو أجبن من <u>نعامة</u>.

Subjects:

1. The enemy is as coward as a <u>cat</u> .
2. The enemy is as coward as an <u>ostrich</u> .
3. The enemy as feeble as an   <u>ostrich</u> .
4. The enemy is as coward as a <u>chicken</u>.
5. The enemy is as coward as a <u>pigeon</u>.
6. The opponent is more coward than an <u>animal</u>.
7. The contender is as coward as a <u>chicken</u>.
8. The foe is an <u>ostrich</u>.

SL ZE	نعامة		
Embedded Image	To show cowardice.		
Sub. No.	Sub. Rs	Arabic-English connotation	The Strategy Adopted
1	Cat	_	Foreignization
2	Ostrich	_	Foreignization
3	Ostrich	_	Foreignization
4	Chicken	+	Domestication
5	Pigeon	_	Foreignization
6	Animal	_	Foreignization
7	Chicken	+	Domestication
8	Ostrich	_	Foreignization

Table (3-5): Comprehensive Analytical Table of Subjects' Translations

<u>**Discussion:**</u>

In Arabic culture there are many symbols of cowardice but the most common of them are (ostrich) which is (نعامة). This animal puts its head in the sand when it is afraid of something thus Arabian people have used such bird to describe a scary person since very long time (Al-Maydani, 2010:245\1). Conversely, this image in English is realized by another animal which is chicken that refer to timid, weak, and cowardly feature (Best, 1958:43). Similarly, Polenova and Klikushina (2014:139) ascribe the same feature, i.e. 'cowardice', to 'chicken' in English culture. Image representation can be shown in the figure below:

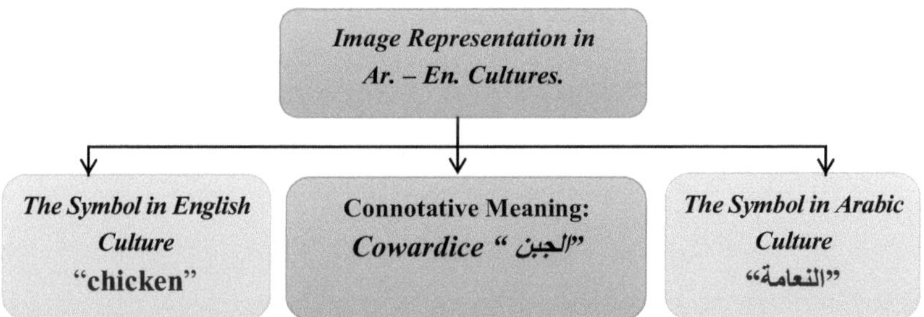

Fig. (3-5): Cowardice Representation in Ar. and En. Cultures.

The translators in their attempt to render the Arabic (ZE) overlooked the difference between English and Arabic cultures and thus they fell in the arena of cultural differences between the two languages. As for subject no. (1), it is incorrect because the image of English word 'cat' cannot be an equivalent to the Arabic (ZE) because it is provided by the rendering, i.e. 'cat' connotes a totally different thing in English, namely 'complacency' (Best, 1958: 85). As for Subjects no. (2, 3, & 8) They are also inappropriate to provide the exact intended meaning by 'نعامة' because they resorted to foreignization strategy and they provided totally strange and not clear images in TL, Since the word 'ostrich' in English does not have the same connotation. Rendering no. (5) is also inappropriate because he/she gave a wrong image (i.e., 'pigeon') which connotes something different from cowardice. Translator no. (6) failed to give the intended meaning but he/she opted for zero – zoomorphic expression. Finally, Subjects no. (4 & 7) are successful in giving the right equivalent with the right connotation by following a domestication strategy and they could convey the exact meaning of the Arabic ZE into English. Thus, the researcher chooses the Subjects of no. (4 & 7) as the most appropriate ones.

<u>The Proposed Rendering</u>:

- The enemy is <u>as coward as a chicken</u>.

<u>ST (6)</u>:

ـ أشأم من <u>غراب البين</u>

<u>Subjects:</u>

1. As worse as seeing <u>a crow</u>.
2. More ominous than the <u>owl</u>.
3. More jinxed than a <u>crow.</u>
4. Seeing dispersed crow makes <u>me luckless</u>.
5. The bird of <u>ill omen.</u>
6. This is like <u>bed omen.</u>
7. More ominous than a <u>swan.</u>
8. Mischievous as a <u>monkey</u>.

SL ZE	الغراب		
Embedded Image	To Express Pessimism		
Sub. No.	Sub. Rs	Arabic-English connotation	The Strategy Adopted
1	Crow	+	Domestication
2	Owl	–	Foreignization
3	Crow	+	Domestication
4	Luckless	–	Domestication
5	Ill omen	–	Domestication
6	Bad omen	–	Domestication
7	Swan	–	Domestication
8	Monkey	+	Domestication

Table (3-6): Comprehensive Analytical Table of Subjects' Translations

<u>**Discussion:**</u>

The image of pessimism is stuck to the 'crow' in Arabic culture because when dwellers leave their house looking for rain water and vegetation the crow comes. It eats from their refusals so they took it as a symbol of pessimism and bad luck because it appears only when they desert their places. So it is named as 'crow of separation'. Therefore, it is said: more ominous than a crow (Al-Maydani, 2010: 284\1).

As for English culture, 'monkey' and 'crow' both refer to pessimism and ill omen (Thomas and Fogen, 2017: 429, 431). Besides, there are other animals which also refer to bad omen such as 'black cat' that is associated with darkness and death (Bradway, 2001: 25). The image can be shown in the following figure:

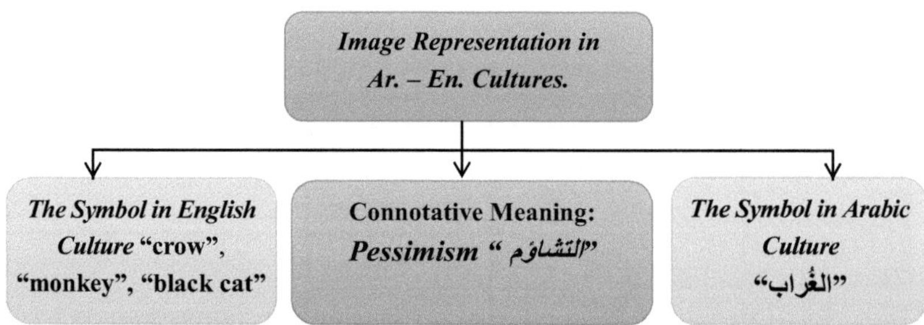

Fig. (3-6): Pessimism Representation in Ar. and En. Cultures.

In Subjects no. (1 & 3), the two translators present appropriate translations for they use the same symbol 'crow' that is used in both cultures. The symbol represents the same image (i.e. bad luck and death) Kindersley (2008: 5). Similarly, Hubbard and Tompkins (2009: 156) mention that crow may represent a symbol of live magic and mystery.

Subject no. (2) is inappropriate because the symbol 'owl' does not refer to pessimism in English culture (Shamah, 2007: 72). In the English culture 'owl' refers to wisdom and virtue (Lews, 2009: 317; Fiore, 2001: 93). For this reason, the mark of 'owl' appears in so many books and references published in the west (Gary, 2007: 145).

Unfortunately, Subjects no. (4, 5 & 6) have not succeeded in giving the appropriate translations because they have not adopted Zoomorphic expressions in formulating sentences.

Subject no. (7) is also inappropriate and has not conveyed the intended image for 'swan' doesn't refer to the pessimism in English culture but rather refers to love. Swan is a symbol for love (Sykley, 2011:79).

Subject no. (8) is inappropriate translation since the subject has transferred the intended image with accurate symbol in the target culture.

<u>Proposed Rendering:</u>

-   It is <u>as spacious as black cat</u>.

<u>ST (7):</u>

- محمّد أسدٌ.

<u>Subjects:</u>

1. Mohammed is a <u>lion.</u>
2. Mohammed is a <u>tiger.</u>
3. Mohammed is a <u>horse.</u>
4. Mohammed is a <u>lion.</u>
5. Mohammed is as brave as a <u>tiger.</u>
6. Mohammed is a <u>brave man.</u>
7. Mohammed is a <u>brave guy.</u>
8. Mohammed is <u>brave.</u>

SL ZE	أسد		
Embedded Image	To express the sense of bravery		
Sub. No.	Sub. Rs	Arabic-English connotation	The Strategy Adopted
1	Lion	+	Domestication
2	Tiger	+	Domestication
3	Horse	+	Domestication
4	Lion	+	Domestication
5	Tiger	+	Domestication
6	Brave man	+	Domestication
7	Brave guy	+	Domestication
8	Brave	+	Domestication

Table (3-7): Comprehensive Analytical Table of Subjects' Translations

Discussion:

The lion, the honorable well-known wild animal. Is as formidable as a King having a special place due to its strength, courage, cruelty, and ferocity. This is why it is an example of ideal power, valor, and gallantry Aashour (2000: 59/1). Lion and tiger also refer to "bravery" in English culture. Lion is commonly shared by both cultures Swinton (1880:17), Phoung & Dung (2016: 20), and Manning and Serpell (1994: 63). *Horse* in another symbol used in Arabic culture Al-Ja'fari (2014:102). The figure below shows the image representation:

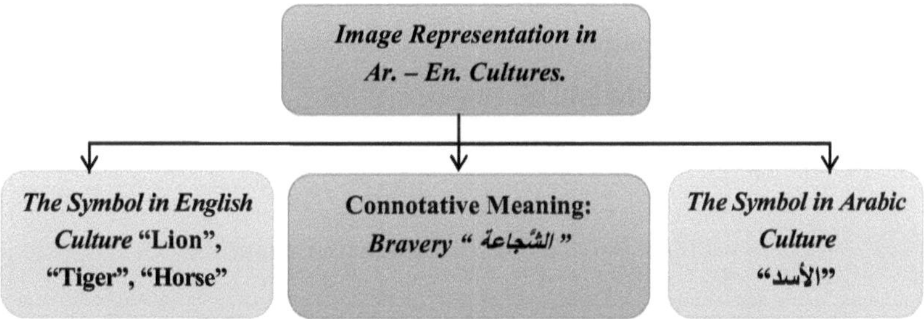

Fig. (3-7): Bravery Representation in Ar. and En. Cultures

Subjects no. (1 & 4) are the most appropriate Subjects for the image has been transferred faithfully. Subjects no. (2 & 5) are also appropriate since they convey the image precisely. As for rendering no. (3), namely 'horse', it is appropriate because this animal also suggests the image of strength, nobility, and courage (Werness, 2006: 220).

Moreover, Subjects no. (6, 7, & 8) are inappropriate because they do not contain Zoomorphic expressions. Finally, 'lion' is the word that accurately convey the intended image as done by subjects (1 & 4).

Proposed rendering:

- Muhammed is a lion.

<u>ST (8)</u>:

- رأيت <u>حمامة</u> في قاعة الأمم.

<u>Subjects:</u>

1. I saw <u>a pigeon</u> at the hall of nation.
2. I witnessed <u>a Musk deer</u> in the hall of nations.
3. I caught a glimpse <u>peace</u> of in the UN hall.
4. I saw a <u>panda</u> at the hall of nations.
5. I saw a <u>nice girl</u> in the hall of nations.
6. I felt <u>peace</u> at the hall of nations.
7. I saw <u>a beautiful person</u> at the hall of nations.
8. I saw <u>a mouse</u> at the hall of nations.

SL ZE	حمامة		
Embedded Image	To convey the meaning of peace		
Sub. No.	Sub. Rs	Arabic-English connotation	The Strategy Adopted
1	Pigeon	_	Foreignization
2	Musk deer	_	Domestication
3	Peace	+	Domestication
4	Panda	+	Domestication
5	Nice girl	_	Domestication
6	Peace	_	Domestication
7	Beautiful person	_	Domestication
8	Mouse	_	Domestication

Table (3-8): Comprehensive Analytical Table of Subjects' Translations

Discussion:

According to the biblical story of the Great flood, the Prophet Nuh (P.B.U.H) sent the dove and it returned to him carrying in her beak a green olive branch. For this reason, 'dove' becomes as a symbol of peace, life, and safety (Bash, 1988: 303). As for English culture, the image of peace is realized by three animals. Therefore, 'musk deer' is considered shy and peaceful animal (Nigam, 2002: 97). 'Panda' is also very common symbol of peace (The Library of Congress, 1973: 5). Similarly, 'musk deer' is another symbol of peace. It can be shown in the following figure:

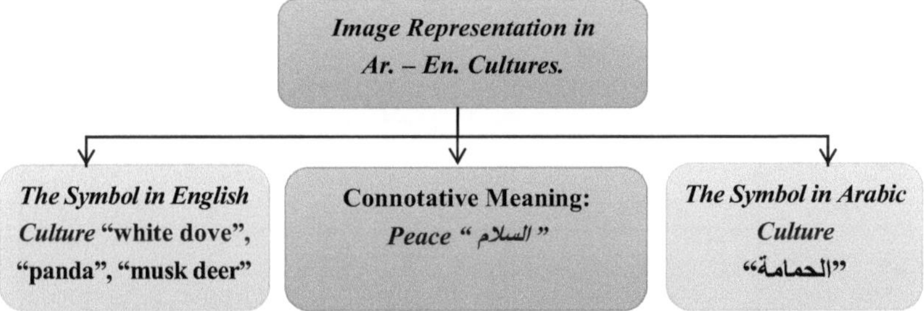

Fig. (3-8): Peace Representation in Ar. and En. Cultures

Subject no. (1) is somewhat appropriate because it denotes to a negative sense (Charless A. Shoemake, 2009: 80; Margo Deme, 2012: 28, 311). 'Pigeons' now represent 'filth' because of their tendency to live in cities and eat human leftovers. Subjects no. (3, 5, 6, & 7) are inappropriate because the translators transferred meaning without zoomorphic expressions (Zero zoomorphic). As for Subjects no. (2 & 4), they are appropriate because the translators are successful when they presented the image giving the suitable equivalent, namely 'musk deer' and 'panda'. Finally, the subject no. (8) is inappropriate because it fails to give appropriate symbol in English cultures. It is clear from what has been previously mentioned that the symbol of 'white dove' is most successful, clear, common and acceptable in both cultures (Palmatier, 1995: 121).

Proposed rendering:

- I saw a person <u>as peaceful as white dove</u>.......

ST (9):

- أزهى <u>من طاؤوس.</u>

Subjects:

1. He is as nice a <u>Carp.</u>
2. As beautiful as a <u>peacock.</u>
3. A pretty as a <u>horse.</u>
4. As beautiful as a <u>moon.</u>
5. More prettier than a <u>peacock.</u>
6. A very <u>nice person.</u>
7. As pretty as a <u>rabbit.</u>
8. More elegant than a <u>bee.</u>

SL ZE	الطاؤوس		
Embedded Image	To show the sense of beauty		
Sub. No.	Sub. Rs	Arabic-English connotation	The Strategy Adopted
1	Carp	−	Domestication
2	Peacock	−	Domestication
3	Horse	+	Domestication
4	Moon	+	Domestication
5	Peacock	+	Domestication
6	Nice person	+	Domestication
7	Rabbit	−	Domestication
8	Bee	+	Domestication

Table (3-9): Comprehensive analytical table of subjects' translations

<u>**Discussion:**</u>

A peacock is a sign of dignity, beauty and splendor, chastity, love and pride in both of the English and Arabic cultures (Al-Damyiri, 1992: 109/3; Al- Maqdissi 2010: 82; Hunt, 2005: 21, 77). However, this image is realized English in by other animals besides 'peacock'. One of which is the 'carp fish' which has long been held in high regard and beauty. Likewise, it's beautifully used on artwork, dress, tattoos, and even in landscape designs (Byghan 2020: 220, 279). 'Horse' is another shared symbol between the two cultures used to achieve beauty and pride (Farahat, 2010: 31; Fox & Mickley, 2012: 90). The following figure shows the image representation:

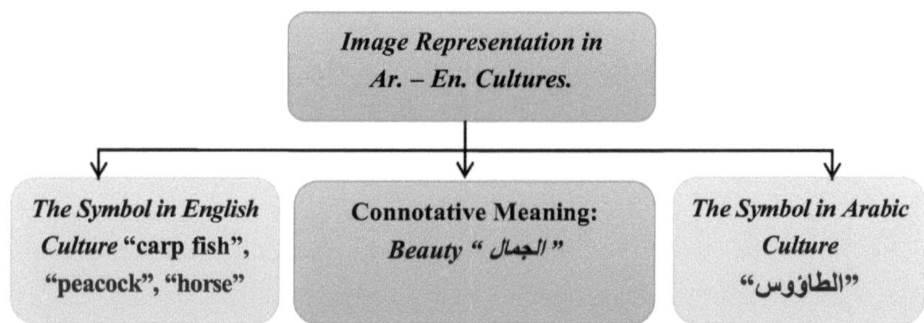

Fig. (3-9): Beauty Representation in Ar. and En. Cultures

Subjects no. (1, 2, 3, and 5) are appropriate since they give the 'equivalent symbol' to achieve the intended meaning that reflect the same effect in the TL culture as it was in the ST. As for Subjects no (4, & 6), they are inappropriate because they may be misunderstood by the TL readers who may not grasp the intended meaning since the expression doesn't contain the basic factor in this study which is ZE without keeping its value in the target text. Although the expressions like 'moon' and 'nice person' reflect somewhat the general meaning but without using Zoomorphic expression.

Subjects no. (7 & 8) are inappropriate since they have resorted to other symbols, namely 'rabbit' and 'bee' since rabbit refers to the abundance and high fertility (Worthy, 2013: 1). Similarly, 'bee' refers to industry, thrift, creative activity and fortune, which are connected with the manufacture of honey (Cirlot, 2013: 52). Finally, the 'peacock' symbol is shared between both cultures, therefore it is nominated to the proposed rendering.

Proposed rendering:

- More prettier than a <u>peacock</u>.

<u>ST (10)</u>:

- ابخل من <u>كلب.</u>

Subjects:

1. Stingier than a <u>dog.</u>
2. It was the <u>cock's egg.</u>
3. The miserable man is like a <u>fattened ox.</u>
4. As stingy person as a <u>pig.</u>
5. He was extremely <u>miser person.</u>
6. He is very <u>stingy.</u>
7. stingy just like a <u>Jew.</u>
8. As stingy as a <u>rooster.</u>

SL ZE	كلب		
Embedded Image	To convey the meaning of stinginess		
Sub. No.	Sub. Rs	Arabic-English connotation	The Strategy Adopted
1	Dog	-	Domestication
2	Cock's eggs	-	Domestication
3	Fattened ox	+	Domestication
4	Pig	+	Domestication
5	miser person	-	Domestication
6	Stingy	+	Domestication
7	Jew	-	Domestication
8	Rooster	+	Domestication

Table (3-10): Comprehensive Analytical Table of Subjects' Translations

<u>**Discussion:**</u>

"Stingier than a dog" is a saying that Arabs used to say about a stingy man or stinginess (Ameen, 1953: 51). Thus, 'dog' becomes an example of stinginess; for the dog, if got something, it never gives up any of it to any other animal of its breed and doesn't accept the partnership of any creature of what it gets of food or drink (Al-tha'alibi, 2005: 54). Therefore, there is a common Arabian saying: "don't ask a bone from a dog" to refer to something impossible to happen (Al-Askari, 1988: 201/1). As for English culture, the matter is somehow different. Therefore, some other animals are used for this image, namely 'stinginess'. 'Pig', as Mallea (2000: 102) states, is widely used in English culture to express the image of stinginess. Likewise, fattened 'ox' is also used as a symbol referring to the mentioned image (i.e., stinginess). 'Rooster' is another animal that is used to express the same image in English culture (Bonwell, 2015: 537, 574). The image can be shown in the following figure:

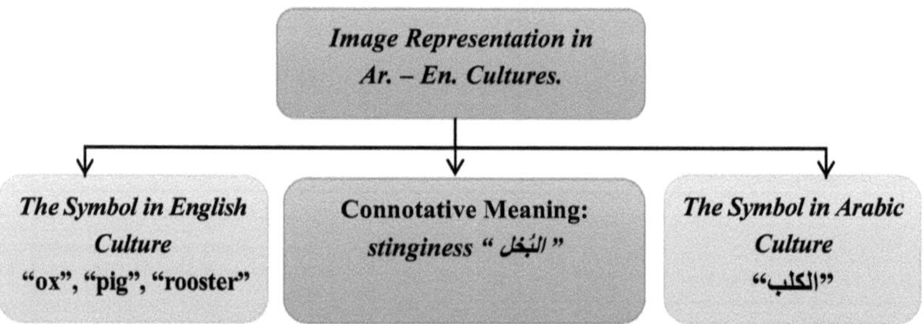

Fig. (3-10): Stinginess Representation in Ar. and En. Cultures

Reviewing the subjects' renderings, one can say that subject no. (1) is inappropriate since 'dog' refers to loyalty and guarding when it wakes the shepherd who may have fallen asleep (Rebecca, 2007: 2). As for sujbect no. (2), who uses 'cock's egg', it is also inappropriate due to the reason that it seems inexpressive about intended meaning. In addition, 'cock's egg' in

English culture does not bring to the mind of the TL reader something equivalent to "ابخل من كلب". Conversely, in Arabic culture, 'cock's egg' refers to the meaning of 'stinginess' (Ibn ManZoor, 2009: 815\2). As for Subjects no. (5, 6, & 7), using 'miser person', 'sting', and 'Jew' respectively, are inappropriate since they do not express the image of stinginess because they lack zoomorphic expressions which we call zero zoomorphic expression. Although, they may express the general meaning of the intended image.

Subjects no. (3, 4, & 8), using *'fattened ox', 'pig', and 'rooster'* respectively, are regarded as appropriate, because the translators have domesticated the intended image bringing the equivalent symbol in the TL with a purpose to make the TL readers familiar with the image in an effective and expressive way.

Proposed rendering:

- Stingier than <u>a fattened ox</u>.

<u>ST (11):</u>

- أجوع من ذئب .

<u>Subjects:</u>

1. More hunger than a <u>wolf</u>.
2. He is <u>starving.</u>
3. He felt the <u>hunger pangs</u> <u>in his stomach</u>.
4. Starving as a <u>bear</u>.
5. Hunger as <u>a church mouse</u>.
6. Hunger as a <u>fasting person.</u>
7. More hunger than a <u>wolf</u>.
8. As hunger as <u>a pig.</u>

SL ZE	ذئب		
Embedded Image	To express the sense of starvation		
Sub. No.	Sub. Rs	Arabic-English connotation	The Strategy Adopted
1	Wolf	+	Foreignization
2	Starving	–	Domestication
3	Hanger pangs in his stomach	–	Domestication
4	Bear	+	Domestication
5	Church mouse	+	Domestication
6	Fasting person	–	Domestication
7	Wolf	+	Foreignization
8	Pig	+	Domestication

Table (3-11): Comprehensive Analytical Table of Subjects' Translations

<u>**Discussion:**</u>

The wolf is a wild animal confident of itself and is considered as the most patient animal that can endure hungry. The disease of wolf is hungry, for it is always hunger. Hence, it represents a symbol of 'hungry'. If the wolf finds nothing to eat, it swallows air and its stomach melts bones. When some people invoke Allah's imprecation upon somebody they say "May Allah inflict him with wolf disease". By this they mean hungry, some people think of it as death (Al-Maydani, 2010: 244/10). It is worth mentioning that the symbol of 'wolf' is shared between both Arabic and English cultures (Gulland, 2011: 48; V&S, 2014: 92). However, besides 'wolf', we have other animals in English culture that signify the image of 'hungry'. One of those animals is 'bear' for it has the feature of 'hungry' (Shaffer, 2014: 12). Similarly, 'church mouse' is also used to denote the image of 'hungry' (Wilstach, 1996: 206). Likewise, 'pig' is another symbol that refers to the image of 'hungry' (Clarke, 2013: 166). The following figure shows the image representation:

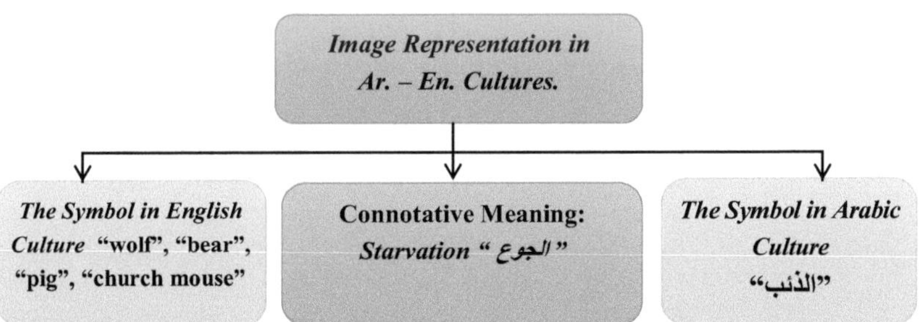

Fig. (3-11): Hungry Representation in Ar. and En. Cultures

Reviewing the above Subjects, one can say that Subjects no. (1, 4, 5, 7 & 8) are appropriate because they used symbols which transfer the expression effectively and accurately retaining the intended image in both cultures in the same force of the original text. Although the translators resorted to formal equivalence, they prefer domestication on foreignization. By so doing, they keep the image of 'hungry' intact for the reader in the target text.

As for Subjects (2, 3, & 6), they are inappropriate because the translators transferred the general meaning of 'hungry' with less expressive force of the message conveyed. In other words, they don't employ animal symbolic language (i.e., zero-zoomorphic expression) which may affect the force of the image, despite the fact that they convey the general meaning.

Proposed rendering:

- As hunger as a <u>wolf</u>…...

<u>ST (12)</u>:

ـ <u>أغدر من التمساح</u>.

Subjects:

1. More treacherous than a <u>hyena</u>.
2. S\he is extremely <u>sly</u>.
3. As treacherous as a <u>fox</u>.
4. A fellow that is more treacherous than a <u>scorpion</u>.
5. More playful than the <u>artful dodger</u>
6. More cunning than a <u>thief</u>.
7. A Man who is more treacherous than <u>the devil</u>.
8. More cunning than a <u>snake</u>.

SL ZE	<u>التمساح</u>		
Embedded Image	To express the sense of treachery		
Sub. No.	Sub. Rs	Arabic-English connotation	The Strategy Adopted
1	Hyena	+	Domestication
2	Sly	−	Domestication
3	Fox	−	Domestication
4	Scorpion	+	Domestication
5	Artful dodger	−	Domestication
6	Thief	−	Domestication
7	The devil	−	Domestication
8	Snake	+	Domestication

Table (3-12): Comprehensive Analytical Table of Subjects' Translations

Discussion:

Alligator is an animal symbolizes power, treachery and deception, as it goes with the saying: "crocodile tears". Living in water and on land, it has become a symbol of the dual nature, namely 'good' and 'evil'. One of the characteristics of this creature is 'treachery' since it attacks other creatures that approach him at lightning speed while hiding underwater, one may see only his eyes (Tharwat, 2012: 164; AL-Dulaimi, 2005: 184). As for the symbol 'Treachery' in English culture, it is realized by a group of animals one of which is 'hyena' (Sax, 2013: 297). Similarly, 'scorpion' reflects the same image (Fagih, 2008: 573; Ferguson, 1961: 24). Moreover, 'snake' is widely used in English culture to suggest the mentioned image (Cresswell, 2014: 279; Qaidar, 2000: 69). Finally, we have 'fox' which also refers to the image of treachery (Varty, 2000: 49). The following figure shows the image in both cultures:

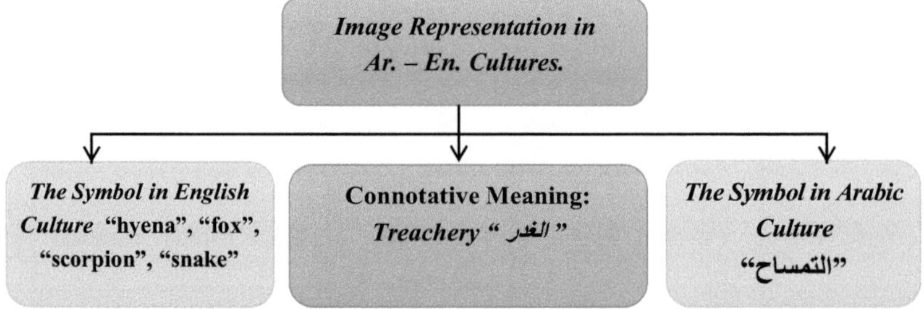

Fig. (3-12): Treachery Representation in Ar. and En. Cultures

The translations in no. (1, 3, 4 & 8) are appropriate ones: 'hyena', 'fox', 'scorpion' and 'snake' respectively. This is because they resorted to domesticate the symbol of the image so that makes the TT. readers grasp the intended meaning of this symbol in his own culture. As for Subjects no. (2, 5, 6 & 7) are inappropriate ones, though they may express the general meaning of 'treachery', Simply because the expressions lack to be in field of zoomorphism, i.e. zero zoomorphic expressions.

Proposed rendering:

-        As treacherous as <u>snake</u> in the grass.

<u>ST (13)</u>:

ـ انت احقد من <u>جمل</u>

<u>Subjects:</u>

1. You are as spiteful as a <u>camel.</u>
2. You are more hateful than <u>anyone.</u>
3. You are a mean <u>man.</u>
4. You are <u>spiteful</u>.
5. You are as hateful as a <u>dog.</u>
6. You are as malicious as an <u>ape.</u>
7. You are as a <u>camel.</u>
8. You are an <u>ox.</u>

SL ZE	<u>جَمَل</u>		
Embedded Image	To show grudge and spitefulness		
Sub. No.	Sub. Rs	Arabic-English connotation	The Strategy Adopted
1	Camel	_	Foreignization
2	Anyone	_	Domestication
3	Mean man	_	Domestication
4	Spiteful	_	Domestication
5	Dog	_	Domestication
6	Ape	_	Domestication
7	Camel	_	Foreignization
8	Ox	_	Domestication

Table (3-13): Comprehensive Analytical Table of Subjects' Translations

<u>**Discussion:**</u>

In Arabic culture, there is perhaps only one symbol for the image 'الحقد' (i.e., 'hatred' or 'spitefulness') which is associated with 'camel' (Al-Askari, 1988: 365). Moreover, camels are actually regarded as very offensive and they are considerably existent in the Arab world (Shora, 2009: 46). Camel doesn't forget the hatred it feels towards somebody for a long time (Al-Zamakhshari, 1962: 30). As for English culture, 'hatred' is an image in animals such as 'Monkey' (V&S, 2014: 116). The image representation can be shown in the following figure:

Fig. (3-13): Spitefulness Representation in Ar. and En. Cultures

Subjects no. (1 & 7) are inappropriate because 'camel' in English culture refers to 'humility', 'willingness' to 'serve', and 'obstinacy' (Anjomshoa & Sadigi, 2015: 16).

Subjects no. (2, 3, & 4) are inappropriate because it doesn't contain a Zoomorphic expression. As for rendering no. (5), it is also inappropriate since 'Dog' in English culture doesn't refer to 'spitefulness', but refers to 'loyalty' and 'guarding' (Nakhavaali, 2011: 5).

Subject no. (6) is inappropriate too. It doesn't convey the intended image because 'ape' in English culture has been used to symbolize 'sin', 'malice', 'cunning', and 'lust'. It may also symbolize the 'slothful soul' of the man, 'blind', 'greedy', and 'sinful' (Ferguson, 1961: 11; Becker, 2000:

20). For this reason, we find 'hatred' trait ascribes to 'monkey' in English culture, Whereas we do not find it in the 'ape', because the translator in Arabic culture has no experience in English culture, So he/she took a generalization in his translation of monkeys without recognizing them or distinguishing between them, but the 'hatred' image in English culture remains in the nature of 'monkey' (Balzac,2018: 218).

Rendering no. (8) fails to capture and convey the intended image, because here the translator chooses the symbol *'ox'*. This symbol doesn't denote to 'hatred' but 'endurance' (V&S, 2014: 1-8).

The proposed rendering:

- As spiteful as <u>monkey</u>.

<u>ST (14):</u>

ـ أظلم من <u>أفعى</u>.

<u>Subjects:</u>

1. 1.Oppressive like a <u>snake</u>.
2. He is unjust.
3. 3.More vicious than a <u>snake.</u>
4. He is an unjust <u>person</u>.
5. He is a <u>bear</u>.
6. He is oppressive as a <u>fox</u>.
7. He is a <u>wasp</u>.
8. He is unjust as a <u>raven</u>.

SL ZE	<u>أفعى</u>		
Embedded Image	To show unjustness		
Sub. No.	Sub. Rs	Arabic-English connotation	The Strategy Adopted
1	Snake	_	Foreignization
2	Unjust	_	Domestication
3	Snake	_	Foreignization
4	Unjust Person	_	Domestication
5	Bear	_	Domestication
6	Fox	_	Domestication
7	Wasp	_	Domestication
8	Raven	_	Domestication

Table (3-14): Comprehensive Analytical Table of Subjects' Translations

Discussion:

According to Arabic culture, this image represents 'unjustness', 'oppression' and 'aggression' which can be materialized in the 'snake'. It is usually said "Deadlier than the snake" which can be used to show how harmful a 'snake' could be. A snake often tries to occupy a hole after forcing its inhabitants to leave their home (hole) to be its own home (Al-Maydani, 2010: 599/2). Another symbol of the mentioned image is 'wolf' for which it is said "more oppressive than a wolf". For this reason, some Arab poets mention in their poems the brutality of the 'wolf' and how it is oppressive and aggressive (ibid.). Conversely, 'spider' in English culture has more than one feature suggesting aggressiveness and cruelty (Cirlot, 2013: 304). The image can be shown in the following figure.

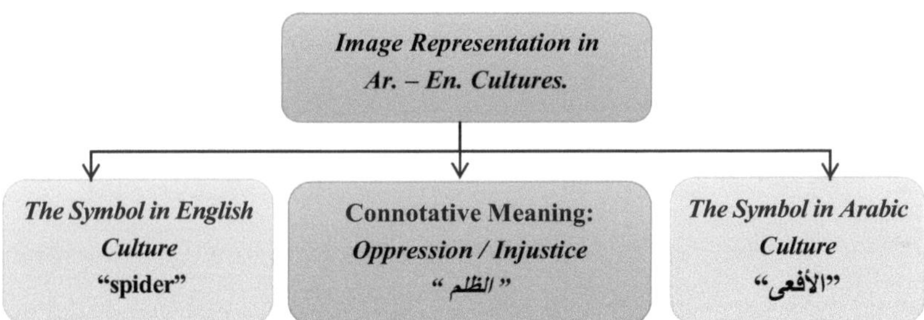

Fig. (3-14): "Oppression" & "Injustice" Representation in Ar. and En. Cultures

Reviewing the above translations, one can say that Subjects no. (1 & 3) are inappropriate since they do not convey the intended image and also 'snake' doesn't refer to oppression in English culture, but point out 'cunning' and 'deceit' (Cross, 2005: 78). As for Subjects no. (2 & 4), they are inappropriate because the two Subjects do not contain Zoomorphic expressions. Furthermore, subject no. (5) is inappropriate too since "Bear" in

English culture does not refer to 'oppression', but symbolize 'hunger' (Best, 1958: 47).

Subject no. (6) is inappropriate since it doesn't capture and convey the accurate image, because 'fox' as a symbol in English culture doesn't refer to 'oppression', but symbolizes 'shrewdness' and 'wit' (Bodenmann & Rey, 2018: 165). Subject no. (7) is also inappropriate because the subject doesn't use precise image, namely 'wasp'. It doesn't refer to 'oppression' in English culture. It symbolizes 'solitude', 'independence', and 'production' (Scazzero, 2017: 37). Finally, rendering no. (8) is also inappropriate because 'raven' does not refer to 'oppression' in English culture. It symbolizes 'war' (Mc Colman, 2003: 79). To domesticate the image to the T.T. Readers, consider the proposed translation below.

<u>Proposed rendering</u>:

- He is as aggressive as a <u>spider</u>.

<u>ST (15)</u>:

ـ أنت عنيد <u>كالبغل</u>.

Subjects:

1. You are as stubborn as a <u>mule</u>.
2. You are an <u>Elephant.</u>
3. You are as obstinate as <u>mule.</u>
4. You are <u>stubborn</u>.
5. You are <u>bull.</u>
6. You are as obstinate as a <u>zebra.</u>
7. You are a <u>tough guy.</u>
8. You are a <u>donkey</u>.

SL ZE	<u>البغل</u>		
Embedded Image	To show stubbornness		
Subjects No.	Sub. Rs	Arabic-English connotation	The Strategy Adopted
1	Mule	+	Domestication
2	elephant	+	Domestication
3	Mule	+	Domestication
4	stubborn	_	Domestication
5	Bull	_	Domestication
6	Zebra	_	Domestication
7	tough guy	_	Domestication
8	Donkey	+	Domestication

Table (3-15): Comprehensive Analytical Table of Subjects' Translations

<u>**Discussion:**</u>

Mules are hybrid animals reproduced by the crossing of a mare with a donkey, While the she-mule is the hybrid by the crossing a horse with a female donkey. The mules are characterized by having the patience of the donkey and the strength of the horse. Mules are characterized by 'stubbornness' in Arabic culture. It is said that "when a mule is forced to carry a very heavy load, it usually throws away its cargo and commits suicide by jumping off a cliff into the deep valley". It is also important to mention that mules are sterile. For this reason, both Odwan (2007:46) and Abdalsaboor (2000:64) agree that 'mule' in Arabic culture is referred to as an animal characterized by 'stubbornness'.

As for English culture the image of 'obstinacy' has a different realization. It is realized by miscellaneous animals. One of which is 'mule' (Allingham, 1968: 93; Edgeworth, 1825: 321). Likewise, 'elephant' is also used to refers to the same image, namely 'stubbornness' Walters, 2018: 331). Furthermore, we have 'donkey' which also refers to 'stubbornness' Finally, 'goat' is the fourth animal that also used as a symbol denoting 'obstinacy' (Lackey, 2003: 106). The following figure shows the representation of the image:

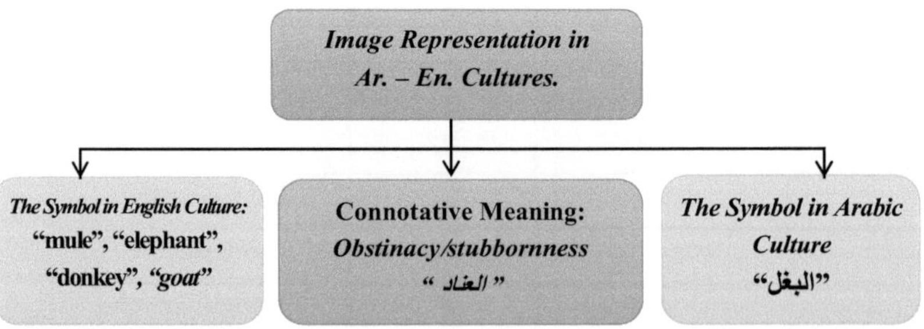

Fig. (3-15): "Oppression" & "Injustice" Representation in Ar. and En. Cultures

<u>**Discussion:**</u>

The Subjects no. (1 & 3) are appropriate because the adopted translation represents the domestication strategy in transferring the intended image given the item 'mule' in both cultures denoting the same image 'obstinacy'. As for rendering no. (2), namely 'elephant', it is also appropriate since it conveys the intended meaning. Subject no. (8) is most appropriate since the word 'donkey' refers to the intended image. Moreover, Subjects no. (4 & 7) are inappropriate because the translators haven't used Zoomorphic expression. Subject no. (5), however, fails to convey the intended meaning since the item 'bull', in English culture, doesn't refer to 'stubbornness' but rather refers to 'power' and 'strength' (Aule, 2002: 662). As for subject no. (6), it is also inappropriate because the expression as 'obstinate as a Zebra' will bring to the mind of the TL Reader something equivalent in meaning between the two cultures, although 'Zebra' doesn't refer to 'obstinacy' in English culture but denotes 'freedom' (Todeschi, 1995: 299). So, we need to domesticate the image to make the TL readers more familiar with the intended meaning in an expressive effective way.

<u>**Proposed Rendering:**</u>

- As obstinate as a <u>goat</u>.

Findings:

The study has come up with certain findings that will be clarified in the charts below:

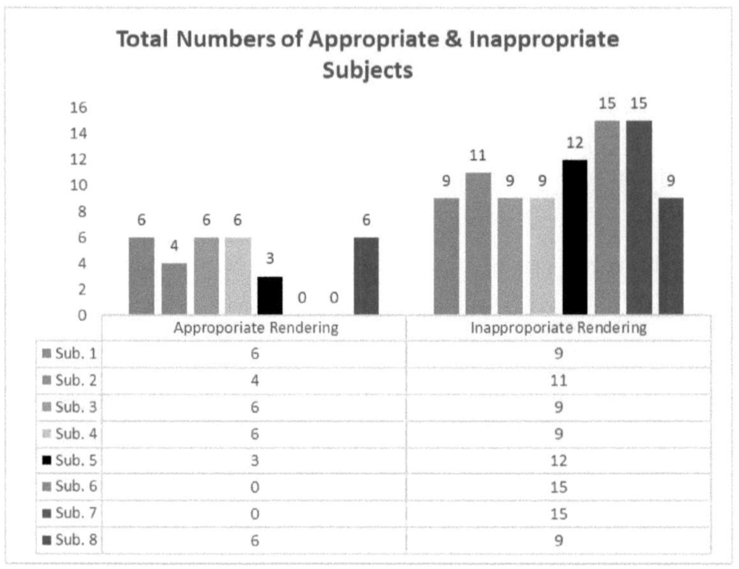

	Approporiate Rendering	Inapproporiate Rendering
■ Sub. 1	6	9
■ Sub. 2	4	11
■ Sub. 3	6	9
▨ Sub. 4	6	9
■ Sub. 5	3	12
■ Sub. 6	0	15
■ Sub. 7	0	15
■ Sub. 8	6	9

Chart (3- 1): Numbers of Appropriate and Inappropriate Subjects

Chart no. (3-1) abovementioned, depending on the procedures that have been followed by the subjects in translating the Arabic ZEs, shows that Sub. no. (1) has (6) appropriate renderings while he/she has (9) inappropriate ones. Likewise, Sub. no. (2) has (4) appropriate renderings and (11) inappropriate ones. On the other hand, Sub. no. (3) has (6) appropriate renderings and (9) inappropriate ones. Similarly, Sub. no. (4) has (6) appropriate renderings and (9) inappropriate ones. As for Sub. no. (5), he/she has (3) appropriate renderings and (12) inappropriate ones. Moreover, all Subjects of both Sub. No. (6 & 7) are inappropriate. Finally, Sub. no. (8) has (6) appropriate renderings while he/she has (9) inappropriate ones.

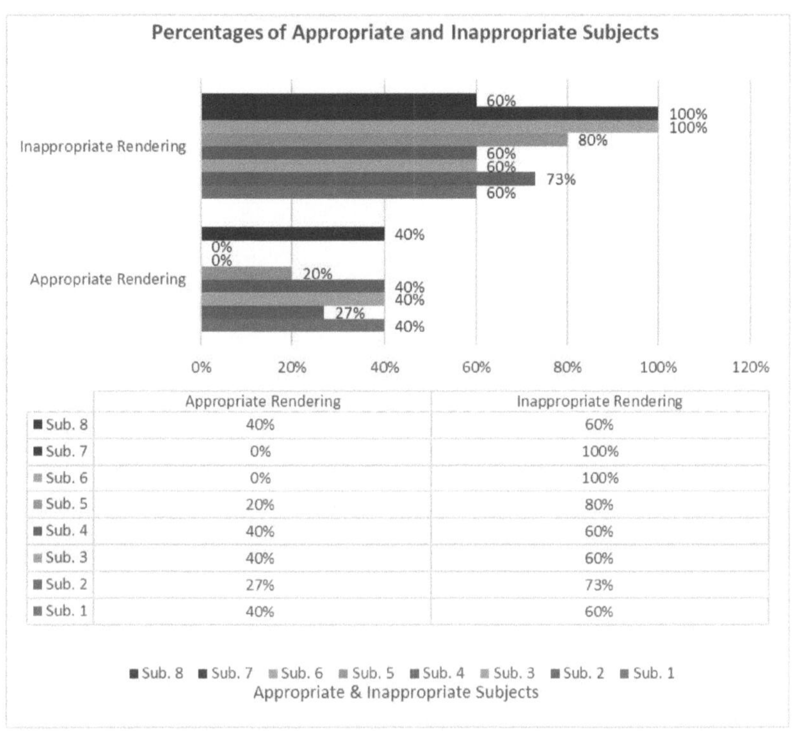

	Appropriate Rendering	Inappropriate Rendering
■ Sub. 8	40%	60%
■ Sub. 7	0%	100%
▥ Sub. 6	0%	100%
▥ Sub. 5	20%	80%
■ Sub. 4	40%	60%
▥ Sub. 3	40%	60%
■ Sub. 2	27%	73%
■ Sub. 1	40%	60%

Chart (3-2): Percentages of Appropriate and Inappropriate Subjects

Chart no. (3-2) above shows the percentages of the appropriate and inappropriate renderings for the all subjects as follows: Sub. no. (1) presented (40%) of appropriate renderings and (60%) of inappropriate ones. Sub. no. (2), on the other hand, achieved (27%) of appropriate renderings and (73%) of inappropriate ones. Likewise, both of Sub. No. (3 & 4) provided (40%) of appropriate renderings and (60%) of inappropriate ones. Moreover, Sub. no. (5) achieved (20%) of appropriate renderings and (80%) of inappropriate ones. As for Sub. No. (6 & 7), both of them failed to present appropriate renderings. Lastly, Sub. no. (8) provided (40%) of appropriate renderings and (60%) of inappropriate ones.

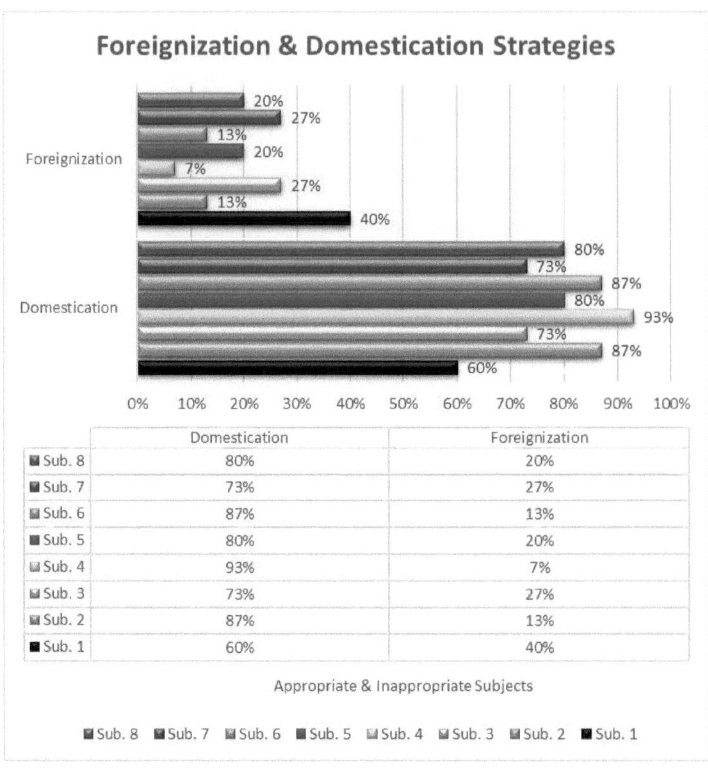

	Domestication	Foreignization
Sub. 8	80%	20%
Sub. 7	73%	27%
Sub. 6	87%	13%
Sub. 5	80%	20%
Sub. 4	93%	7%
Sub. 3	73%	27%
Sub. 2	87%	13%
Sub. 1	60%	40%

Chart (3-3): Foreignization & Domestication Strategies

Chart no. (3-3) shows the translation orientation of each subject (i.e., the percentages of foreignization and domestication strategies used by each subject). Sub. no. (1) followed (40%) of SL oriented and (60%) of TL oriented. Sub. no. (2), on the other hand, went after (13%) of SL oriented and (87%) of TL one. Likewise, Sub. no. (3) used (27%) of SL oriented and (73%) of TL one. Moreover, Sub. no. (4) made use (7%) of SL oriented and (93%) of TL one. As for Sub. no. (5), he/she handled (20%) of SL oriented and (80%) of TL one. Sub. no. (6) followed (13%) of SL oriented and (87%) of TL oriented. Additionally, Sub. no. (7) made use (27%) of SL oriented and (73%) of TL one. Finally, Sub. no. (8) went after (20%) of SL oriented and (80%) of TL one.

The most dominant translation strategy used in translation ZEs in the study is Domestication (80%). Foreignization, by contrast records only (20%). It is a very good coincidence that the study highly recommends the same strategy provided that it achieves the intended image in TL. Subjects no. (1, 3, 4 and 8) are the best among others students in producing the intended meaning of the given Arabic ZEs via providing the SL counterpart items and adopting the appropriate strategy.

S. N.	ZEs in Arabic Culture	ZEs Representation in English Culture	Proposed Rendering	Figurative genre
1.	رأيت ذئبا يتناول العشاء في المطعم.	The camel is a symbol used in English culture to refer voracious.	As voracious as a camel eating his meal at the restaurant.	Metaphor
2.	كيف يمكنك السير لمسافات طويلة دون ان تشرب الماء فعلا أنك سفينة صحراء.	The ox is a symbol used in English culture to refer patience.	You are really as patient as an ox.	Metonymy
3.	قنافذ الليل منبوذة من الجميع ولا يحبها احد.	The blackbird is a symbol used in English culture to refer gossip.	No one likes a blackbird	Metonymy
4.	يبدو أن أبا الاخبار لم تحمله جناحيه الينا اليوم فبتنا لا نعلم ما يدور حولنا	The Hoopoe is a symbol used in English culture to refer with power of sight.	The little bird seems.	Metonymy
5.	العدو أجبن من النعامة	The chicken is a symbol used in English culture to refer cowardice.	The enemy is as coward as a chicken	Simile
6.	أشأم من غراب البين	The Black cat is a symbol used in English culture to refer pessimism.	As spacious as black cat	Simile
7.	محمد اسد	The lion is a symbol used in English culture to refer bravery.	He is a lion	Metaphor
8.	رأيت حمامة في قاعة الامم	The white dove is a symbol used in English culture to refer peace.	As peaceful as white dove	Metaphor
9.	أزهى من طاووس	The peacock is a symbol used in English culture to refer beauty.	More prettier than a peacock	Simile

S. N.	ZEs in Arabic Culture	ZEs Representation in English Culture	Proposed Rendering	Figurative genre
10.	أبخل من كلب	The <u>dog</u> is a symbol used in English culture to refer <u>stinginess</u>.	More stingier than a <u>dog</u>	Simile
11.	أجوع من ذئب	The <u>wolf</u> is a symbol used in English culture to refer <u>hungry</u>.	As hunger as a <u>wolf</u>	Simile
12.	أغدر من التمساح	The <u>snake</u> is a symbol used in English culture to refer <u>treacherousness</u>.	As treacherous as <u>snake</u> in the grass	Simile
13.	أنت أحقد من جمل	The <u>monkey</u> is a symbol used in English culture to refer <u>spitefulness</u>.	As spiteful as a <u>Monkey</u>	Simile
14.	أظلم من أفعى	The <u>spider</u> is a symbol used in English culture to refer <u>oppressiveness</u>.	He is as aggressive as <u>spider</u>	Simile
15.	عنيد كالبغل	The <u>goat</u> is a symbol used in English culture to refer <u>stubbornness</u>.	As obstinate as a <u>goat</u>	Simile

Table (3-16): Total Description of Data under Study

CHAPTER FOUR

CONCLUSIONS, RECOMMENDATIONS AND SUGGESTIONS FOR FURTHER STUDIES

4.1 Conclusions:

This study has come up with the following conclusions:

1. The phenomenon of Zoomorphism exists in English and Arabic, but one-to-one equivalence is less common since the two languages belong to different language families. Thus, the same sense is expressed in English via another zoomorphic expression.

2. Extra-linguistic elements, cultural conventions and customs, for instance plays a vital role in representing the linguistic items and expressions like ZEs.

3. Animal word does not only denote to the animal physical entity but also has deep-rooted socio-cultural connotations in both cultures. This leads to linguistic incongruity as an essence of the dissimilarity across cultures, namely, Arabic and English.

4. Translators, readers and leaners are required to have a deep perception of zoomorphic expressions, to recognize the heavy-laden connotations words. Only profoundly familiarizing with the cultural customs as well as conventions, people could communicate and interact with English-tongue communities successfully and self-confidently.

5. Culturally speaking, although sometimes a speaker may use a hyponymy item that belongs to the same animal, the symbolism remains different. See e.g.: Dove –pigeon.

95

6. Culturally speaking, some pairs of ZEs have the same denotations, but different connotations. Although sometimes a speaker may use an animal symbol that belongs to the same animal family, the symbolism remains without difference. For example: Monkey- Ape/Eagle-Falcon/Scorpion-Snake/Crow- Raven.

7. Some images are realized by more than one symbol. For instance, the image of "stubbornness" or "obstinacy" in English culture. It could be represented by more than one symbol, namely: (Mule, Goat, Elephant and Donkey)

8. A symbolic relationship may be found between socio-cultural environment and a symbol that results in ZEs such as church mouse in English Culture and Camel in Arabic culture.

9. It may happen that one symbol has a shared image between two cultures. For example, the symbol lion has the image of bravery in Ar. and En. cultures. In the same way the symbol ostrich can also be used to represent an image of fear and cowardice.

10. For generating a satisfactory translation of the SL text ZEs, it seems very important to produce the similar effects on the TL readers as those of the SL readers.

11. Since the majority of the Arabic ZEs are culture-specific, the students committed serious mistakes when they resorted to literal translation to put these ZEs into English. In several cases, the students resorted to the formal equivalence by keeping the SL ZEs as such to save the cultural flavor of SL, consequently the resultant translation was unacceptable by TL readers.

12. When we translate we do not only convey the linguistic elements but also we convey the culture of the SL. into TL. The norms of the SL. must have equivalents in the target language otherwise the translation will lose its cultural flavor and color. Overlooking TL. Culture leads in many cases to awkward translation and foreign one. It may seem very strange to the TT readers.

4.2 Recommendations:

The study puts forward the following recommendations:

1. For producing an acceptable translation of the original text AEs, it seems very important to recreate the identical or at least the comparable effects on the target language audience as those experienced by the SL readers.

2. Translation students should be familiar with the cultural differences between Arabic and English and the role played by culture in the process of translation.

3. Decision making is very important in the process of translation, accordingly, translation students must be familiar with the strategies and procedures of translation in order to make the right decision when they translate.

4. English/Arabic have several rhetorical devices that enrich the language and gives it its specificity. Zoomorphism is one of these culture-specific terms that requires special knowledge on the part of the student, thus translation students should be acquainted with such figurative use of the language.

4.3 Suggestions for Further Studies:

1. The study suggests investigating the problems of translating ZEs in sports as the nicknames given to sportsmen and sport women.

2. It is suggested to make an assessment of Arabic translation of animal symbolism in English literary text, for instance, ZEs in Animal Farm by George Orel.

3. It is also proposed to investigate the difficulties of translating English derogatory ZEs texts by the president of USA (Trump) on social communication media.

REFERENCES

Aashour, A. (2000). **Mawsoo'at At-Tayr wal-Hayawan fil-Hadeeth Ash-Shareef**. University of Michigan: Maktabat al-Quran.

Abdul-Saboor, S. (2000). **Ma'saat al-Hallaj**. Maktabat al-Eskandariyah.

Abdulwahid, Y. & Ibrahim, H. (2011). Formal and Functional Meanings in the Glorious Qur'an with Reference to Translation. In: **College of Basic Education Researchers Journal**. Vol.11, No.3. The University of Mosul.

Agha, M. (1994). **Honorification**. University of California. Los Angeles PP.277-302.

------------ (2001). **Aspects of Cultural Significance in the English Translation of Tayber Salih's "The Doum Three of Wad Hami"** Adab Al- Rafidayn. Vol.34.

Al- Damyiri, K. (1992). **Hayat Al-Hayawan Al-Kubra**. Min Al-Turath Al-Arabi.

Al- Jabri, M. (2006). **The Problem of Equivalence in English Arabic Translation: Towards Apractical Framework of Creative Equivalence in Arabic**. Unpublished PhD. Thesis.

Al-Askari, A. (1988). **Jamharat al-Amthal**. Lebanon, Beirut: Dar Al-Kutub Al-Ilmiyyah Lil-Nashr wat-Tawzee'.

Al-Dulaimi, S. (2005). **Aalam Al-Ahlam: Tafseer Ar-Rumooz wal-Ishaaraat**. Beirut: Dar Al-Kutub Al-Ilmiyyah.

Al-Ja'fari, A. (2014). **Ana fi Shi'r Al-Mutanabbi**. Algeria: Ministry of Culture.

Allingham, M. (1968). **Cargo of Eagles.** 1st ed. UK., London: Vintage, Chatto & Windus.

Al-Maqdissi, E. (2010). **Kashf Al-Asrar fi Hikam At-Tuyoor wal-Azhaar**. Revised by: Mohamed A.A., Dar Al-Fadheelah.

Al-Maydani, A. (2010). **Majma' al-Amthal**. Vol. 1. 3rd ed. Lebanon, Beirut: Dar Al-Kutub Al-Ilmiyah.

Al-Qadhi, R. (2020). **Istid'aa' Ash-Shakhsiyyat At-Ta'reekhiyyah fi ash-Shi'r al-Abbassi hatta Nihayat al-Qarn al-Raabi' al-Hijri**. Jordan, Amman: Al-Abdali, Ministry of Culture, Dar Al-Khaleej for publishing and distribution

Al-Sulaiman, M. (2011). **Semantics and Pragmatics.** Mosul: Dar Ibn Al-Atheer.

Al-Tha'alibi, A. (2005). **Thimar al-Quloob fil-Mudhaaf wal-Mansoob**. Dar al-Kutub al-Ilmiyah.

Al-Zamakhshari, A. (1962). **Al-Mustaqsa fi Amthal Al-Arab**. 1st ed. Wazarta al-Ma'arif lil-Tahqeeqaat al-Ilmiyah wa-ath-Thaqafiyah lil-Hukoomah al-Hindiyah.

Ameen, A. (1953). **Qamoos al-'Adaat wal-Taqaleed wat-Ta'abeer al-Masriyah**. Matba'at Lajnat at-Ta'leef wat-Tarjamah wan-Nashr.

Anjomshoa, L. & Sadighi, F. (2015). The Comparison of connotative Meaning in Animal Words between English and Persian Expressions and their Translation. In: **International Journal on Studies in English Language and Literature**. Vol. 3. Issue, 2. Iran, Sheraz & Kerman: Islamic Azad University. pp. 65-77.

Ashley, M. (2009). **The Arts of Learning and Communication: A Handbook of the Liberal Arts**. Wipf and Stock Publishers.

Auel, M. (2002). **Los Refugios de Piedra (Shelters of Stone)**. Vol 5. Earth's Chidren, Libros en Espanol Series.

Aziz, Y. and Lataiwish, M. (2000). **Principal of Translation**. Benghazi: Garyounis university press.

Aziz, Y. (1982). **Culture problems of English - Arabic Translation**, Bable, Vol, XXV III; No.1:25-29.

Baker, M. (2003). **Routledge Encyclopedia of Translation Studies**. Shanghai Foreign Language Education Press.

Balzac, H. (2018). **The Comedy of Human Life**. B A Books.

Barker, C. (2003). **Cultural Studies: Theory and Practice**. 2nd Ed. London: Sage Publications Ltd.

Bash, H. (1988). **Al-Mu'taqadat Al-Sha'biyya fi Al-Turath Al-Arabi: Dirasah fi Al-Juthoor Al-Istooriyya wal-Deeniyya wal-Maslakiyya Al-Ijtima'yya**. Dar Al-Jaleel.

Bassnett, S. (2004). **Translation Studies**. Shanghai: Shanghai Foreign Language Education Press.

Becker, U. (2000). **The Continuum Encyclopedia of symbols**. New York & London: Continuum.

Berko, et al. (1992). **Communicating** (5[th]ed). USA, Pennsylvania: Pennsylvania University Press. Cengage Learning.

Best, D. (1958). **The Students' Companion** (2[nd]ed). UK., Glasgow: Collins Clear – Type Press.

Bodenmann, S. & Rey, A. (Eds.). (2018). **What Does it Mean to be an Empiricist? Empiricisms in Eighteenth Century Sciences**. Switzherland, Zurich: University of Zurich. Springer.

Bonwell, R. (2015). **Rodgers Dictionary of Proverbs**. London: Rodger Bounty Books.

Bradway, K. (2001). Symbol Dictionary: Symbolic Meanings of Sandplay Images. In: **Journal of Sandplay Therapy/ Sandplay Therapists of America**. Retrieved from: www.sandplay.org.

Brislin, R. (1976). Introduction in Translation. Gardner press,Inc, Newmark:1-43.

Byghan, Y. (2020). **Sacred and Mythological Animals**. USA.: Library of Congress and British Library.

Catford, J. (1965). **A Linguistic Theory of Translation**. London: Oxford University Press.

Çepýk, Ş. (2006). Positive Neutral Negative Evaluation in Connotation. In: **IBSU International Refereed Multi-Disciplinary Scientific Journal**. No. 1. pp.: 144-147.

Chandler, D. (2002). **Semiotics: The Basics**. USA, New York: Routledge.

Childs, P. & Fowler, R. (2006). **The Routledge Dictionary of Modern Critical Terms**. New York: Routledge Taylor & Francis Group.

Cirlot, E. (2013). **A Dictionary of Symbols** (2nded). USA., New York: Philosophical Library, courier Corporation.

Clarke, J. (2013). **The Face of the Father**. Balboa Press.

Cresswell, J. (2014). **Little Oxford Dictionary of Word Origins**. Oxford: Oxford University Press.

Cross, G. (2005). **Worktowners at Blackpool**. Routledget.

Crystal, D. (2003). **A Dictionary of Linguistics & Phonetics**. London: Basil Blackwell Inc.

Cui Xuena, W. Y. (2015). **A Study on Cultural Connotation of Animal Words in English and Chinese.** Qinhuangdao Institute of Technology, Qinhuangdao City, Hebei Province, China Yinggang066100@163.com.

Demello, M. (2012). **Animals and Society: An Introduction to Human-animal Studies**. Colombia University Press.

Edgeworth, M. (1825). **works**. vol. IX. Washington – Street, Boston.

Ezzat, A. (1993). **Language and Culture in Translation.in Seminar papers**. First Series on Creativity in Translation. Cairo:CDELT, Ain Shams university.

Fagih, A. (2008). **5 Novels**. USA., Scorpions & Vipres.

Farahat, S. (2010). **Dilalat Al-Haywan wat-Tayr fi Ash-Shi'r Al-'Ebri Al-Andalussi fil-Qarnain Al-Haadi 'Ashar wa Ath-Thaani 'Ashar Al-Miladiyain**. University of Ciaro, Eastern Studies Center.

Ferguson, G. (1961). **Signs and Symbols in Christian Art**. London: Oxford University Press.

Fiore, J. (2001). **Symbolic Mythodology**. USA: Writers Club Press.

Fløistad, G. (2005). **Philosophical Problems Today**. University of Oslo: Kluwer Academic Publishers.

Fox, W. & Mickley D. (2012). **Advances in Animal Welfare Science**. USA, Washington, DC.: University of Wisconsin / Madison, Springer Science & Business Media.

Fudge, E. (2010). **Renaissance Beasts: Of Animals, Humans, and Other Wonderful Creature**. USA: University of Illinois Press.

Gary, R. (2007). **Creatures in the Mist**. USA.

Ghazala, H. (2002). **Translatability of Cultural Terms (English- Arabic): Translation Mechanisms**. Turjuman, Vol. 11, 67-90.

Greenberg M. & Harman G. (2005). **Conceptual Role Semantics**. Princeton University.

Gulland, M. (2011). **English as Easy as ABC**. Berlin: Grada Publishing.

Hatim, B. & Mason, I. (1990). **Discourse and the Translator**. London: Longman.

House, J. (1977). **A Model for Translation Quality Assessment**. Tubingen: Gunter Narr.

Hu, K. & Hye, K. (2019). **Corpus-based Translation and Iterpreting Studies in Chinese Contexts**. Palgrave Macmillan.

Hubbard, S. & Tompkins, D. (2009). **Witch School: Living the Wiccan Life**: Wicca and Paganism Series. LIewellyn Worldwide.

Hunt, L. (2005). **Animals Divine (Companion)**. USA., Minnesota: Llewellyn Publications.

Hurtado, A. (2001). **Translation and Translation Studies: Introduction to Translation Studies**. Madrid: Cátedra.

Ibn Manzoor, J. (2009). **Lisaan al-'Arab**. Beirut: Dar Al-Kutub Al-Ilmiyah.

Ibrahim, A. (2013). **Riwayat Gharbia Ean Rihlat fi Shubh Aljazira Alarbia 1900-1952**. Beirut: Dar As-saaqi lilnashr.

Ilyas, A. (1989). **Theories of Translation**. Iraq, Mosul: Mosul University Press.

Kim, L. (1996). **Caged in Our Own Signs: A Book about Semiotics**. Vol. (55). USA, New Jersey: Ablex publishing corporation Norwood.

Kindersley, D. (2008). **Signs & Symbols**: An Illustrated Guide to Their Origins and Meanings. Dorling Kindersley Ltd.

Knutsen P. et al. (2012). **Narratives of Risk: Interdisciplinary Studies**. Germany, Stfold University College, Waxmann Verlag GmbH, Münster 2012.

Lacey, R. (1996). **A Dictionary of Philosophy**. London: Routledge .

Lackey, M., Flint, E., & Freer, D. (2003). This Rough Magic, Mercedes Lackey. USA, Production by Windhaven Press, Auburn. NH.

Littlemore, J. (2015). **Metonymy. Hidden Shortcuts in Language, Thought and Communication**. Cambridge: Cambridge University Press.

Liu, J. (2013). A Comparative Study of English and Chinese Animal Proverbs –From the Perspective of Metaphors. In: **Theory and Practice in Language Studies**, Vol. 3, No. 10, pp. 1844-1849. Academy Publisher Manufactured in Finland.

Lyons, John. (1981). **Language and Linguistics**. Great Britain: Cambridge University press.

Mallea, J. O. (2000). **Speaking Through the Aspens**. Reno, Nev: University of Nevada Press.

Manning, A. & Serpell, J. (1994). **Animal and Human Society: Changing Perspectives**. 1st ed. London: Routledge.

Mc Malcolm, K. (2003). **Phrasal Analysis: Analyzing Discourse Through Communication Linguistics**. India, Chennai: Replika Pvt Ltd.

Mieder, W. (1996). **Proverbium: Yearbook of International Proverb Scholarship**. Finland, Helsinki: DeProverbio.com.

Nakhavali, F. (2011). **A Semantic and Cultural Study of Animal Expressions in English and Persian**. Iran, Mashhad: Ferdowsi University of Mashhad.

Nancy, B. (2018). **Zoomorphism**. Retrieved from: https://doi.org/10.100//s10670-018-0088-0.

Newmark, P. (1982). **Approaches to Translation**. London: Prentice Hall International Ltd.

------------- (1988). **A Textbook of Translation**. UK. Prentice Hall International Ltd.

------------- (1991). **About Translation**. Multilingual Matters.

------------- (2001). **Context in translation**. Amsterdam, Philadelphia: John Benjamins Publishing Company.

Nida, E. & Taber, C. (2003). **The Theory and Practice of Translation**. Boston. Brill

Nida, E. (1964). **Linguistic and Ethnology in Translation – Problems**. In Dell Hymes (ed). Language in Culture and Society.

---------- (2002). **Contexts in Translating**. Vol 41. Benjamins Translation Library, John Benjamins Publishing.

Nigam, D. (2002). **Tourism Environment and Development of Garhwal Himalaya**. India, New Delhi.

Nolan, J. (2005). **Interpretation: Techniques and Exercises, Professional Interpretation in the Real World**. Multilingual Matters.

Odwan, M. (2007). **Haiwanat Al-Insan**. Damascus: Dar Mamdooh Odwan Lil-Nashir wa At-Tawzee'.

Oliver, D. & Lewis, J. (2009). **The Dream Encyclopedia**. Visible Ink Press.

Omeysh, H. & Malkishi, W. (2015). **Dilalat al-Hayawan fil-'Amthal ash-Sha'bia alqbaylyia fi mintaqat bani mlkish – bjayt – a semantic study**. unpublished M.A. Thesis. Algeria: University of Abdul-Rahman Mira Bejaia-

Osipian, L. (2018). **Political and Economic Transition in Russia Predatory Raiding, Privatization Reforms, and Property Rights**. USA, Madison: University of Wisconsin.

Pagani, G. et al. (2014). **Metaphor and Intercultural Communication**. USA, New York: Bloomsbury Publishing.

Palmatier, R. (1995). **Speaking of Animals: A Dictionary of Animal metaphors**. USA: Greenwood Publishing Group.

Palmer, R. (1976). **Semantics**. Combridge University Press. Great Britain. London.

Phuong, T. & Dung, V. (2016). The Similarities and Differences in the Connotation of Animal Words in English and Vietnamese Proverbs. In: **European Journal of English Language Teaching**. Vol., 1. Vietnam, Trang City: University of Khanh Hoa, Nha. Retrieved from: www.oupub.org/edu.

Plotkin, V. (2006). **The Language System of English**. Universal Publishers.

Polenova, T. &   Klikushina, G. (2014). **Collected Articles of the 3rd International Linguistics Conference.** Russia: Taganrog.

Qaidar, F. (2000). **The Translation of English Animal metaphors into Arabic: A cognivitve-Pragmatic Perspective**. Unpublished MA. Thesis, University of Mosul.

Radden, B. et al. (2007). **Aspects of Meaning Construction**. John Benjamin's Publishing Company.

Radhakrishna, S. et al. (2012). **The Macaque Connection: Cooperation and Conflict between Humans and Macaques**. Vol. (43). India, Kyoto University.

Rashidian, Z. (2014). **Representing the Modern Animal in Culture**. USA, New York: Palgrave Macmillan.

Rasul, S. (2019). **Journalistic Translation: Procedures and Strategies in English - Kurdish Translation of Media Texts.** Cambridge: Cambridge Scholars Publishing.

Rebecca, C. (2007). **Horse People: Thoroughbred Culture in Lexington and Newmarket**. Baltimore, Maryland: The Johns Hopkins University Press.

Sax, B. (2013). **The Mythical Zoo: Animals in Myth, Legend, and Literature**. USA., New York: The Overlook Ress Duck Worth.

Scazzero, T. (2017). **Power Animals and Their Symbolism**. Lulu Press, Inc.

Seely, J. & Shakespeare, W. (2005). **Much Ado about Nothing**. Heinemann.

Seleskovitch, D. & Lederer, M. (1984). **The Interpretive Theory of Translation**. Paris: Didier Publication.

Shaffer, J. (2014). **Grizzly Bear**. USA., North Mankato, Minnesota: Core Library.

Shamah, Kh. (2007). Al-Boom Ramzul Tashaa'um fi Al-thaqafi Al-Arabiya, in: **Al-Thaqafiyah**. Vol. 66. pp. 71-72.

Shoemake, A. (2009). **Apotheosis of My butterfly**. Xlibris Corporation.

Shora, N. (2009). **The Arab-American Handbook: A Guide to the Arab, Arab-American & Muslim Worlds**. Cune Press, Seattle.

Shuttleworth, M. & Cowie, M. (2004). **Dictionary of Translation Studies**. Shanghai: Shanghai Foreign Language Education Press.

Skilja, D. (2013). **1001 Idioms to Master Your English: Everyday English Idioms**. Retrieved from: www.trafford.com North America & international (USA & Canada)

Steiner, G. (1975). **After Bible: Aspects of Language and Translation**. USA, Oxford University Press.

Swinton, W. (1880). **Masterpieces of English Literature**. USA., Washington: The Office of the Librarian of Congress.

Sykley, J. (2011). **The Twilight Symbols: Motifs – Meanings – messages**. CPI Group (UK) Ltd., Croydon.

Tanesini, A. (2007). **Philosophy of Language A – Z**. Edinburgh: Edinburgh University Press Ltd .

Tharwat, A. (2012). **Taj Al-Hudhud, Novel**, Al-Dar Al-Masriyya Al-lubnaniyya.

The Library Progress, (1973). **Works of Art**. Washington: The Library of Congress. Washington: The Library of Congress.

Thomas, E & Fogen, T. (2017). **Interactions Between Animals and Humans in Graeco-Roman Antiquity**. UK., Durham University, Walter de Work

Todes, P. (2014). **Ivan Pavlov: A Russian Life in Science**. New York: Oxford University Press.

Todeschi, J. (1995). **The Encyclopedia of Symbolism**. Berkley Publishing Group. University of California.

Toury, G. (1995). **Descriptive Translation Studies and Beyond**. Amesterdam: John Benjamin's Publishing Company.

V. & S. Publishers (Eds.). (2014). **Concise Dictionary of Metaphors & Similes**. New Delhi: Param Offseters Okhla.

Vallely, A. et al. (2012). **Animals and the Human Imagination: A Companion to Animal Studies**. Columbia University Press.

Varty, K. (Ed.). (2000). **Reynard the Fox: Social Engagement and Cultural Metamorphoses in the Beast Epic from the Middle Ages to the Present**. USA., New York: Berghahn books.

Venuti, L. (2004). **The Translation Studies Reader** (3rded). USA and Canada, Routledge.

Walters, E. (2018). **Elephant Secret**. New York: Rule of Three Inc.

Webster, M. (1984). **Merriam Webster's Dictionary of Synonyms**. Merriam Webster, Inc.

Werness, B. (2006). **The Continuum encyclopedia of animal symbolism in art.** New York: Continuum.

Wilstach, F. (1996). **A Dictionary of Similes**. Toronto: Thomas A.T.T. Pen Publisher.

Worthy, B. (2013). **Totem Animal Messages**. Balbo Press.

Yusuf, A. (1989). **The Holy Quran: Text, Translation and Commentary**. Printwood, M? Amana Co. retrieved from www.islam101.com.

مقدمة الكتاب

التعاملُ مع التَعبيراتِ الخاصَّةِ بالحَيْوانِ (الدلالات الحَيَوانِيَّةِ) أصْعبِ المَجالاتِ التداولية في التَرْجميَّةِ. ولا شكَّ أنَّ كلَّ ثقافةٍ تستعملُ لُغَتَها بِطريقةٍ تَعْتَمدُ فيها على مَجموعةٍ مُتَنَوِّعةٍ مِنْ العَواملِ مِثْلُ التقاليدِ، والافكار الفَلْسَفِيَّةِ، والأنْشِطة اليَوميَّةِ، والانظمة الاجتماعِيَّة ، وما إلى ذلكَ. إنَّ استعمالَ اللّغةِ للتَعبير عن العَالمِ حَوْلَنا يَخْتَلِفُ مِنْ لُغةٍ إلى أخرى، وخاصَّةً في استعمالِ دلالاتِ الحَيوانِ: ومِنْ هُنا تنشأ المُشْكلةُ فيكونُ لِكلِّ تَعْبيرٍ كمّ دلاليٍّ مُكوَّنٍ مِنْ أكثر مِن مَعْنى يَكونُ مُتَغيراً ثَقافياً في حينٍ لا يَعلم المُتَرجمُ هل يجب عليه أنْ ينقلَ بصورةٍ مُباشرةٍ ما يُقالُ أوْ يُكتبَ إلى اللّغةِ الهَدَفِ أويتحقّقَ مِنْ ثَقافةِ تِلْكَ اللّغةِ لإيجادِ التَناقضِ والتَشابهِ بَيْنَ الثّقافةِ المَنقولِ مِنْها والمَنْقولِ إليها مِنْ أجْلِ تَوْفيرِ صورةٍ مُناضِرةٍ مُناسِبةٍ . هذه الدِراسةُ هي مُحاولةٌ لِسدِّ تِلْكَ الفَجوةِ الثَّقافية.

تَهْدفُ هذه الدِراسةُ بِشكلٍ رَئيسٍ إلى: (1) تَقْديم دِراسةٍ شامِلةٍ للتَّعبيراتِ الخاصّةِ بالحَيوان باللغتينِ الانكليزية والعربية ، (2) اختبارِ قدرة المُتَرجمينَ في تَرْجمةِ التَعبيراتِ الخاصّةِ بالحَيوان المُخْتَلفةِ ثقافياً وجينياً مابينَ الثَّقافتينِ (3) اظهار اختلاف دلالةَ هذه التَعْبيراتِ في اللّغةِ الأمِّ (العربية) تَخْتَلِفُ عَنْ تِلكَ المَوجودةِ في اللّغةِ الانكليزية (اللّغةِ الهدفِ) . (4) الكَشْفِ عَنْ أسْبابِ الاختلافاتِ بَيْنَ دلالاتِ اسماء الحيوانيةِ مابينَ اللغتينِ العربيةِ والانكليزيةِ ، و(5) تحديدِ أساليبِ التَرجمةِ التي استعملها المترجمون والصعوباتِ التي واجهوها.

ولِتحقيقِ هذه الأهدافِ ، افترضتِ الدِّراسةُ أنَّ (1) التَّعبيراتِ الخاصة بالحَيوانِ في اللّغةِ العربيةِ لا يُمْكِنُ تَرْجمتُها بِنَجاح إلى اللّغةِ الانكليزيةِ دونَ استيعابِ القِيمِ الثَّقافيةِ والاختلافاتِ والأصولِ الموروثة لكلِّ ثقافةٍ (2) تَجاهلَ الاختلافِ الثَّقافيِّ بَيْنَ اللّغتينِ يُؤدي إلى تراجم غير مَفْهومةِ ، (3) اتخاذَ القرارِ الجَيّدِ مِنْ جانبِ المُتَرْجمينَ يُساعِدُ وبشكلٍ جدُّ كبيرٍ في التَوصّلِ إلى ما تَعْنيه التَعْبيراتُ الحَيُوانيةُ التي تَكونُ مرتبطةً بِثقافةِ اللّغة الأمِّ.

لاختبارِ صحةِ هذه الفَرضياتِ ، قامَت الدراسة بمايأتي: (1) أخذِ عَيِّنةٍ مُتكونةٍ مِن 15 مِثالاً مِن اللّغةِ العربيةِ التي تَحْتَوي على تَعْبيراتٍ مُتَعلقةٍ بالحَيوانِ مُشْتقةٍ مِنْ مُخْتَلفِ الكُتبِ العَربيةِ الأصيلةِ التي تُعنَى بِبلاغةِ اللّغةِ (2) هذه الأمْثلةُ تَمَّتْ تَرْجمَتُها مِنْ قِبلِ 8 طلبةٍ (طلبة ماجستير في قسم الترجمة /كلية الاداب/ جامعة الموصل)، (3) تَصنيفِ هذه التَعابيرِ مِنْ حَيثُ نَوعُها المَجازيُّ ، أي"التشبيه، الكناية والاستعارة"

أمَّا الاستنتاجاتُ الرئيسةُ التي تَوصَّلتْ إليها الدِراسةُ فَهي (1) إنَّ عَدمَ وجودِ خَلْفيةٍ ثقافيةٍ لدى الطَّلبةِ أدى إلى سُوءِ فَهمِ تِلْكَ التعابيرِ ومما أدى الى ترجمتِها بشكلٍ خاطىٍ، (2) نَقلُ صورةِ اللّغةِ الأمِّ إلى اللّغةِ الهَدفِ دونَ أيِّ اعتبارٍ لِغيابِ التَداخلِ الثَّقافيِّ بَيْنَ اللغتينِ مِما أدى إلى تَرجمةٍ خاطِئةٍ (3) وكانت اعلى نِسبةٍ لاستعمالِ التَرجمةِ التقريبيةِ (25) حالة وبنسبةٍ (%20) مُقابِلَ التَرجمةِ التَّعريفيةِ (95) حالة وبِنسبةٍ (%80) تَكشفُ أنَّ غالبيةَ الطَّلبةِ غيرُ مُدْركينَ للاختلافاتِ الثَّقافيةِ بَينَ اللغتينِ والتي تُؤدي دوراً هاماً جداً في عملية الترجمة.

تنتهي الدِراسةُ إلى بَعضِ التَّوصياتِ المُتَعلقةِ بطرق التعليم وبَعضِ الاقتراحاتِ لإجراءِ دِراساتٍ أخرى.

I want morebooks!

Buy your books fast and straightforward online - at one of world's fastest growing online book stores! Environmentally sound due to Print-on-Demand technologies.

Buy your books online at
www.morebooks.shop

Kaufen Sie Ihre Bücher schnell und unkompliziert online – auf einer der am schnellsten wachsenden Buchhandelsplattformen weltweit! Dank Print-On-Demand umwelt- und ressourcenschonend produzi ert.

Bücher schneller online kaufen
www.morebooks.shop

KS OmniScriptum Publishing
Brivibas gatve 197
LV-1039 Riga, Latvia
Telefax: +371 686 204 55

info@omniscriptum.com
www.omniscriptum.com

Printed by Books on Demand GmbH, Norderstedt / Germany